ArtScroll Series®

Rabbi Nosson Scherman / Rabbi Meir Zlotowitz

General Editors

WORDS OF WISDOM
WORDS OF WIT

WORDS OF WISDOM

Published by

Mesorah Publications, ltd

WORDS
OF WIT

A veritable storehouse of Jewish experience — its honey and spice

by Shmuel Himelstein

FIRST EDITION
First Impression . . . October 1993

Published and Distributed by
MESORAH PUBLICATIONS, Ltd.
Brooklyn, New York 11232

Distributed in Israel by
MESORAH MAFITZIM / J. GROSSMAN
Rechov Harav Uziel 117
Jerusalem, Israel

Distributed in Australia & New Zealand by
GOLD'S BOOK & GIFT CO.
36 William Street
Balaclava 3183, Vic., Australia

Distributed in Europe by
J. LEHMANN HEBREW BOOKSELLERS
20 Cambridge Terrace
Gateshead, Tyne and Wear
England NE8 1RP

Distributed in South Africa by
KOLLEL BOOKSHOP
22 Muller Street
Yeoville 2198, South Africa

Typography by Compuscribe at ArtScroll Studios, Ltd.

Printed in the United States of America by Noble Book Press
Bound by Sefercraft, Quality Bookbinders, Ltd. Brooklyn, N.Y.

To Judy

An ideal wife,
exceptional teacher,
and mother extraordinary —
not only to our children and grandchildren,
but to countless students
from all over the world
who have been adopted by
and have adopted her
as their "second mom."

ואת עלית על כלנה

ᦾ Contents

◆§ The Community

◆§ Jewish Thought

Introduction

When I first started collecting stories for the first volume of this series, *A Touch of Wisdom, A Touch of Wit*, I soon realized the tremendously rich diversity and quantity of stories about our greatest sages. The first volume was soon filled, and there was more than enough which I would have liked to include, but for which there was simply no room. This, then, is another, entirely different collection of stories of the *gedolim*.

What did I look for? First — and I cannot deny it — the story had to be appealing to me. The different stories had their own appeal — some proclaimed a deep Torah truth which should be of relevance to all of us in our daily lives. (Take for example, the story of the *Chazon Ish* walking deliberately slowly behind a man with a limp, not to have the man feel his infirmity so keenly.) Some stories taught the proper way to think or to act. (R' Moshe of Kobrin felt that a person should never feel that things are bad. They may be bitter — just as the medicine a sick person needs may be very bitter indeed — and taking it is for the person's good.) Others made me smile or even laugh out loud. (R' Eizel Charif proved to a *maskil* that the youngest of children knew the answer to a basic arithmetic question, while the *maskil* did not — the question being what day of the *Omer* it was.) In the final analysis, then, each story had to have a certain appeal, and, indeed, each one did to me. I can but hope that you, the reader, will agree with my choices.

I should mention one phenomenon I came across periodically in my work. There have been a number of instances not very many — where I have found the same identical story — attributed to different people. Obviously, there is no way at this stage to identify who was actually involved. As long as the story had a valid message I decided to include it, hoping that the attribution which I cited was indeed correct. I sincerely believe that the message is, in the final analysis, what is most important to us. Let us hope that the messages of these stories come through, so that we may hopefully learn from them.

Between Man and God

Prayer

✍§ *A Logical Argument*

R' Moshe Leib of Sassov used to pray: "Hashem, You state clearly in Your Torah that if a person finds something which is lost, he is to look after it until the owner reclaims it. It is already close to two thousand years that we have been 'lost,' exiled from our land. We therefore beg and beseech You to come and search for us! It is time for You to reclaim Your lost object — the Jewish people."

✍§ *A Prayer by R' Levi Yitzchak*

R' Levi Yitzchak of Berdichev once addressed Hashem on Shavuos as follows: "Hashem, on Rosh Hashanah You are our King, and the *halachah* is that a king may not forgo the honor due him. On Shavuos, however, when we celebrate Your giving of the Torah, You are our *Rav*, and the rule is that a *rav* has the right to forgo the honor due him. That being the case, I beg You to forgive all our sins against You and grant us a full pardon."

◄§ How to Judge One's Fear of Hashem

The *Yehudi Hakadosh* once explained to his son the meaning of the verse, "And you were tired and weary and did not fear Hashem" (*Devarim* 25:18): "If you are tired and weary after having prayed, that is a clear sign that you do not fear Hashem, for one who fears Hashem becomes stronger from his prayer."

◄§ Never the Same Twice

R' Yisrael of Vizhnitz saw one of his young chassidim trying to mimic the way he acted and prayed. "It's a waste of time for you to try to copy me," he told the young man, "because my prayer today is different from my prayer yesterday."

◄§ No Fear

R' Zvi Hirsh of Safrin once told a young man who had just led the prayers with perfect vocal virtuosity, "You cannot serve here as the *chazan* again. Anyone who doesn't have even the smallest trace of fear when *davening* before the congregation is suspect of not having fear before Hashem either."

◄§ Pray for the Right Thing

R' Naftali of Ropshitz once told the following story. "During the siege of Sebastopol, Czar Nicholas I was saved from certain death when a burly private kicked his horse and made it bolt out of the way of a bullet headed directly for his heart.

Later, the Czar beckoned the private and asked him what reward he desired. 'Your majesty,' replied the private, 'our sergeant is a cruel man. Could you please replace him with another sergeant?'

" 'Fool,' replied the Czar, 'why did you not ask me to make you a sergeant?'

"The same is true with us," concluded R' Naftali. "We pray to Hashem for such small things, when we should be praying for the main thing — that Hashem bring us our redemption."

⋗§ Save Us From Bankruptcy

R' Yechezkel of Kozmir once beseeched Hashem: "Hashem, our debt to You is very great. When a businessman is in danger of bankruptcy, his creditors extend him yet more credit in the hope that his situation will improve and he can pay them off. Similarly, we ask of You to 'write us in the book of life' — grant us a little more credit — 'for Your sake' — so that we will be able to repay the debts we already owe You."

⋗§ Please Pick Up the Tefillin

R' Shlomo Lenchner once prayed: "Hashem, You know that if a Jew drops his *tefillin*, he picks them up, kisses them, and fasts because the *tefillin* carry Your name. We are told that You, too, wear *tefillin*, in which it states, 'Who is like Your people Israel, a unique nation in the world?' Your people are lying on the ground, trodden upon by all. Would it not be proper for You to pick them up and send deliverance to them?"

⋗§ Your Tefillin Are Not Valid

R' Levi Yitzchak of Berdichev used to say: "Hashem, unless you forgive the sins of Your people Israel, I will reveal a secret: You are wearing invalid *tefillin*. After all, we are told that Your *tefillin* carry the words, 'Who is like Your people,

Israel, a unique nation in the world?' If You do not forgive us, we will not be a unique nation, and You, as it were, will be making a mockery of that which is written in Your *tefillin*."

◄§ Your Wish Will Be Granted

R' Shmuel of Kariev explained *Chazal*'s statement, "Everything is from Heaven except fear of Heaven," as follows: "When a person prays to Hashem, his request may or may not be granted. That is what is meant by 'everything is from Heaven' — everything is at Hashem's discretion. There is but one exception to this rule — a person who prays for fear of Heaven will definitely have his prayer granted."

◄§ No Permission Is Necessary

The second morning after R' David Kronglas, *mashgiach* of Ner Israel in Baltimore had a massive heart attack, his wife came to visit him early in the morning. Seeing him *davening* in his *tallis* and *tefillin*, despite still being in intensive care, his wife asked him whether he had sought the doctors' permission. R' David replied in amazement, "Why should I ask them? Do I need to ask them whether I am permitted to breathe? Why, then, should I need their permission to put on my *tallis* and *tefillin*?"

◄§ Yours Not to Reason Why

A man who had been in pain for many years asked R' Simchah Bunim of Pshischa if he was permitted to recite the daily morning blessing, "*She'asah li kal tzorki* — Who has given me all my needs." Might such a blessing not be a *berachah levatalah* — a blessing in vain — as far as he was concerned?

R' Simchah Bunim answered, "Your need is to accept your suffering without complaint. Thus, when the Torah states, 'You shall be pure (*tamim*) with Hashem' (*Devarim* 18:13),

Rashi interprets this to mean that you should accept whatever lot Hashem gives you without question."

✍ We All Come Together

A certain *gadol* once remarked, "It is true that the chassidim and misnagdim have a different order for the *Shacharis* prayers, but when they get to *Yehi Chevod* — 'May Hashem's glory endure forever and ever' — they all come together, and all work for the same goal."

✍ What Right Have I?

One of the Gerrer Rebbes came upon hard times. His wife, knowing of how he always prayed for others who came to him with their needs, suggested that maybe just this once he should pray to Hashem and ask His help for the family.

"That I will not do," replied the Rebbe. "I am required to do Hashem's will, but what right do I have to ask Him to do my will?"

✍ A Reasonable Supposition

R' Shmuel of Lubavitch demanded of his chassidim that they think holy thoughts as they went about their business. One of his chassidim complained that the Rebbe expected them to do something impossible. "I assume," R' Shmuel replied, "that if you are capable of profane thoughts during the *Shemoneh Esrei*, you are capable of holy thoughts while working."

✍ It Depends for What You Ask

R' Uri of Strelisk, known as the *Seraf*, lived his entire life in great poverty. His chassidim once asked him why some Rebbes were so wealthy while he was so poor.

"It's very simple," replied R' Uri. "The rule is that if a person prays to Hashem on someone else's behalf, and he also needs that for which he is praying, he is answered first. Some rebbes have chassidim who ask them to pray that they become wealthy. When the Rebbe prays for them, and he, too, needs money, Hashem sends it to him first. My chassidim, however, ask me only to pray that they become truly pious Jews. Since I also need this, Hashem helps me serve Him with all my heart and soul."

Proper Belief

⊰ *A Difference of Opinion*

The brothers R' Elimelech and R' Zushia had a major disagreement. R' Elimelech believed that a person should first work on recognizing his own insignificance. Once one truly recognizes his insignificance, he can begin to understand the greatness of Hashem. R' Zushia, on the other hand, believed that a person should work on recognizing the greatness of Hashem, and thereby come to recognize his own lowliness. When their rebbe, the *Maggid* of Mezritch, was asked about which of the two views was right, he replied, "Both ways lead to the same goal, but R' Elimelech's view is superior to that of R' Zushia."

⋅§ A Different Standard

In Bialystok there lived a wealthy miser, who would, for appearance sake, occasionally invite a poor man to his home for a meal. But once there, the poor man would receive only bread and water.

R' Moshe Ze'ev, the *rav* of the town, summoned the miser to see him. The man defended himself against R' Moshe Ze'ev's sharp criticism: "The Torah states, 'You shall love your neighbor as yourself,' and I can assure you that I, myself, don't eat any more than I give these poor people."

"While you might have learned once," said R' Moshe Ze'ev, "you evidently overlooked something in your studies. The *Gemara* tells us that the angels asked Hashem why He favors the Jewish people over the other nations. Hashem replied, 'How can I not favor them? I commanded them, "You shall eat and be satisfied and bless Hashem," but they are more stringent upon themselves and thank Me, without being satiated, after eating only an olive-sized piece of bread'. Why does the *Gemara* state that they are stringent *upon themselves*? Could it not state simply, 'they are stringent?' This teaches us that a person can be stringent only upon himself, but when it comes to feeding the poor, he has to give them enough so that they can 'eat and be satisfied.' "

⋅§ A Foreign God

R' Menachem Mendel of Kotzk was asked, "Rebbe, what did King David mean when he wrote in *Tehillim*, 'You shall have no strange (*zar* in Hebrew) god'? After all, the Torah already tells us that 'You shall not have any other gods.' "

"What David meant to teach us," said R' Menachem Mendel, "is that Hashem should not be a stranger (*zar*) to you, but should be within you always."

A Lazy Man

R' Yitzchak Meir of Gur said of a certain person: "He does not have true *bitachon* in Hashem. He is simply too lazy to think things out, and his *bitachon* is the easy way out for him."

A Lesson From the Giving of the Torah

R' Yisrael Salanter said, "The Torah was given to the Jewish people in an unknown place — in the middle of a desert — and at an unknown time — on either the sixth or the seventh of *Sivan*. This teaches us that the Torah applies in all times and in all places, and not, as people frequently claim, that it is impossible to observe the Torah where they live or that the Torah's commandments must be adapted to the times and brought up to date."

Actions Speak Louder Than Words

"If a person repeats a thousand times, 'You shall bind them on your hands,' he still does not fulfill the *mitzvah* of *tefillin* unless he physically places the *tefillin* on his hand," said the *Chafetz Chaim*. "Similarly, if a person repeats a thousand times, 'You shall love Hashem your God,' that is not enough unless he arouses his heart to really love Hashem."

At a Time Like This?

R' Yichiel Michel of Zlotov lived in great poverty, and both he and his family suffered constant want and hunger. His chassidim asked him, "Rebbe, why don't you pray to Hashem for relief from your poverty?"

"Let me tell you a story," the Rebbe answered. "Once there was a mighty king with a daughter whom he loved dearly. When the time came for his daughter's marriage, the king sent wedding invitations to all the prominent people in the kingdom.

"On the wedding day, the daughter became very ill. Her life was in danger, and the wedding was called off until she recovered. All the guests went home — except for one. This man insisted that he had traveled a long way and was entitled to partake of the wedding feast. He was served a full meal, but all who saw him looked upon him with disdain.

"The same is true of me," said R' Michael. "Ever since the *Beis Hamikdash* was destroyed, the *Shechinah* has been in exile. Every night we arise at midnight to lament that fact. At such a time, how can I bother Hashem with my small needs?"

✑ Believing in Hashem

A great *talmid chacham* was sitting with his *talmidim*, when he suddenly asked them, "Do you believe in Hashem?" For a second they were all taken aback, but then a powerful chorus of "Yes" echoed around the table. After all, the students pointed out, "Each morning we recite that Hashem is our God, Hashem is One."

"That's very interesting," said the *rav*, "because I don't believe in Hashem." As his students whispered to one another, "How can our teacher not believe in Hashem?" he continued. "Do you all *believe* that you are sitting next to a table? Obviously not. You all *know* that you're sitting next to a table. And by the same token, when I look around me at the sun, moon, and stars — everything in this wonderful world of ours — I don't *believe* in Hashem, I *know* that He rules the world."

✑ Don't Forget

R' Yisrael Salanter used to say, "When one recites the *Shema* and thinks that Hashem is God over all four corners of the universe, he must not forget that He is also God over him."

⋅§ "Es" Is Inclusive

As is known, R' Akiva interpreted every usage of the word אֶת in the Torah to include something not explicit in the Torah. For example, when the Torah states that we must fear "אֶת Hashem," R' Akiva learns that the word אֶת includes Torah scholars. Similarly, the Baal Shem Tov deduced from the verse, "You shall rebuke [אֶת] your friend," that before rebuking anyone else, one must first rebuke himself.

⋅§ Heed Your Words

R' Chaim of Volozhin explained the words in *Pirkei Avos*, "*Chachamim* take care with your words," to mean that a person who wishes to rebuke another must be sure that his words do not apply equally to himself. If a person is himself free of blemish, his words are accepted much more readily.

⋅§ Even "Oh" Is Superfluous

In Lublin there lived a pious, learned Jew, who also happened to be very wealthy. He owned large forests from which his men cut down trees and floated the logs to Danzig to sell them there. The *dayan* of the town, on the other hand, was extremely poor. For some reason, the wealthy man loved to tell the *dayan* that money is of no importance; the main thing is to be grateful for whatever one has and not complain about his lot. After all, he said, *Chazal* tell us that one must thank Hashem as much for the bad as we thank Him for the good.

Once, a storm destroyed an entire shipment of logs on its way down the river. The question now arose as to how to break the news to the merchant. No one wanted to bear the bad tidings, and in the end it was decided that the *dayan* should do so.

The *dayan* entered the merchant's home and started talking about various matters. Sure enough, the merchant soon came around to discussing the importance of thanking Hashem for the bad as well as the good.

Casually, as it were, the *dayan* asked the merchant, "Do you think that you could really live by that saying?"

"Of course," said the merchant. "I have no doubt on that score."

"Well then, I'm sorry to break the news to you that your entire shipment to Danzig was destroyed," said the *dayan*.

The merchant paled before his eyes, and gave out a single cry, "Oh!"

"Even that single 'Oh!' is superfluous,' said the *dayan*.

From that time on, there was an expression in Lublin, "Even a single 'Oh!' is superfluous."

⇜ False Torah Cannot Be Allowed to Exist

R' Chaim Brisker did not write down his own Torah *chiddushim*. Rather he had R' Noach, a *shochet* who was also a fine *talmid chacham*, record his *chiddushei Torah*.

One *motzaei Shabbos,* R' Chaim asked R' Noach to come to him and take notes. R' Noach came, and R' Chaim started dictating — hour after hour, with only a short break to give R' Noach some rest. When R' Noach had filled twelve full pages of notes, R' Chaim decided that everything he had said was wrong. He immediately asked R' Noach for the sheets and began tearing them up. "But Rabbi," said R' Noach, "I, too, can tear up the pages."

He answered R' Noach, "False Torah is not permitted to remain in the world for even the extra instant it would have taken to tell you to tear it up."

⇜ For Whom the Sun Shines

R' Yisrael Salanter very much enjoyed the sunshine. He once said, "Each of us should be very grateful for the sunshine, but man's nature is such that generally he is only grateful for those things which only he enjoys and others do not."

⋙ Foretelling the End of Days

The *Yehudi Hakadosh* used to say: "How can anyone claim to reveal when the End of Days will come? That is meant to remain a secret. Indeed, if anyone reveals that secret, it's a clear sign that he doesn't know it!"

⋙ Happy With One's Lot

The author of *Kli Yakar* used to say: "Our Sages do not state, 'Who is wealthy? He who is *satisfied* with his lot,' but rather 'He who is *happy* with his lot.' This teaches us that it is not enough for a person to be satisfied with what he has; he must be happy with what Hashem decreed for him, regardless of his circumstances."

⋙ Hashem Keeps His Word

The *Chafetz Chaim* told the story of a poor widow who lived in Radin. She was unable to pay her rent, and the landlord tried to evict her. When the local people prevented this, the landlord brought in a bunch of thugs, who simply removed the roof of the widow's home, leaving her exposed to the elements.

"I remembered this incident," said the *Chafetz Chaim*. "I believed that Hashem, protector of widows, would undoubtedly hear the widow's cry. A number of years passed, and the man continued to live a tranquil life. I couldn't understand it. Was Hashem making a travesty of His Torah, which states, 'My anger will be kindled, and I will kill you' against those who oppress a widow?

"Ten years after the widow was evicted, the landlord was bitten by a rabid dog. He was infected with rabies, and soon began barking like a dog. Soon afterwards, he died a horrible death."

◆§ Hashem's Uniform

R' Chaim of Sanz was once awakened in the middle of a nap by a loud knocking on the door. When he opened it, he was taken aback. Standing before him was a soldier holding a warrant for his arrest. It soon became clear that an error had been made and the warrant was for someone else.

Later, R' Chaim commented, "It is interesting how, when a simple peasant wears the uniform of the Czar's army, we are all terrified of him. If we would wear the uniform of Hashem's army — the *tallis* and *tefillin* — all nations would fear us in the same way."

◆§ How Eliyahu Arrives

R' Menachem Mendel of Kotzk once sent one of his chassidim to open the door at the *Seder* to recite *shefoch chamascha* — "pour out Your wrath." As he approached the door, the chassid froze in fright. When asked why he was so frightened, the chassid replied, "I'm sure, Rebbe, that Eliyahu himself must be waiting at your door."

"You're wrong," said the Rebbe. "Eliyahu enters through the heart, not through the door."

◆§ How Much Fear One Needs

R' Menachem Mendel of Kotzk once asked one of his chassidim if he had ever seen a wolf, and whether he had been afraid. "Rebbe," replied the chassid, "I did indeed once see a wolf, and I was very much afraid."

"And were you aware that you were afraid?" continued the Kotzker. "No, Rebbe," said the man, "I was too frightened to realize that I was afraid."

"That," said the Kotzker, "is how much fear of Heaven a person should have. He should be so fearful that he does not even realize that he is afraid."

⊷ How to Approach Hashem

The *Maggid* of Mezritch used to say, "Many people make the mistake of believing that Hashem is in the highest heights, and that if a person wishes to approach Him, he has to ascend upward. The opposite is true. Hashem seeks those who are truly humble and lowly, those who pour out their hearts to Him in humility. The more a person brings himself down, the more he humbles himself, the closer he is to Hashem."

⊷ How to Live Long

R' Shimon of Yaroslav lived to a ripe old age. When his *talmidim* asked him to what he attributed his long life, he answered, "I always accepted everything which happened to me with love, and I never questioned Hashem's actions. If a person questions Hashem's actions, he is brought up to Heaven and shown that everything is just. Since I never complain, there was no need to take me to Heaven to see that all of Hashem's actions are just."

⊷ I Learned Two Things

R' Leibele Eiger was a chassid of the Kotzker Rebbi. When he returned home after an extended stay with the Kotzker, his father asked him what he had learned in Kotzk. "I learned, Father," replied R' Leibele, "that even though a man is a man and an angel is an angel, through his deeds a man can become greater than an angel. And I learned, 'In the beginning, Hashem created' — but then He wants man to 'help Him' in creation."

◄§ I, Too, See It

A wealthy merchant came to R' Chaim of Volozhin for advice. "Rabbi," he said, "I have a very large shipment of wood which is being held up at the border by the customs officials. Unless it can be brought through, I stand to lose everything I own."

"Trust in Hashem," said R' Chaim, "for He will help."

Meanwhile, the price of wood jumped, and by the time the shipment had been cleared through customs, its value had skyrocketed. The merchant made thousands of rubles additional profit because of the delay.

Rushing to R' Chaim, the merchant told him, "Rebbe, now I know that Hashem is directly involved in our daily affairs!"

"In that," said R' Chaim, "you differ from the poor. The poor see Hashem's involvement each day, while the rich see it only at rare intervals."

◄§ If I Were Hashem

"If I were Hashem," began R' Shneur Zalman of Liadi.

"Yes? What would you do?" all asked eagerly.

"If I were Hashem," said R' Shneur Zalman, "I would run the world exactly as Hashem does."

◄§ It Depends on How You Sleep

The first section of the *Shulchan Aruch*, *Orach Chaim*, discusses the need to get up in the morning "like a lion, to serve one's Creator." On this, the *Rama* comments: "When one lies down, he must know before Whom he lies down."

"This comment seems out of place," said R' Meir of Premishlan. "It should come in Section 239, which discusses going to sleep. There is, however, a reason it is placed here. If that person goes to sleep like a horse, will he get up in the morning like a lion? If a person goes to sleep like a horse, he will wake up like a horse. That is why the *Rama* stressed specifically here that one must know before Whom he is going to sleep."

⊸§ It Depends on the Question

A man came to R' Yehudah Asad for advice. "Rebbe," he said, "I want to buy a certain run-down store, which will give me the opportunity to support my family and myself comfortably. What do you suggest?" R' Yehudah told him not to buy the store.

The next day, another man came to ask R' Yehudah for advice. "Rebbe," he said, "if I buy this store, I will, with the help of Hashem, be able to fix it up and earn a decent living." This time, R' Yehudah urged the man to go ahead.

When the first man heard R' Yehudah's advice to the second, he grew furious and ran to him. "Rebbe," he said, "yesterday I asked you about buying that same store, and you told me not to. Why did you tell the other man to buy it?"

"It's very simple," said R' Yehudah. "You wanted to take on the task of running a run-down store all by yourself, and I felt that it was too much for one person. The other man, on the other hand, stated, 'with the help of Hashem.' With a partner like that, I felt that he has an excellent chance of making a go of it."

⊸§ It's a Prayer

R' Noach of Lechovich once heard one of his chassidim beginning to recite the *Rambam's* Thirteen Principles of the Faith. "I believe with perfect faith," the man began — and stopped. Again he repeated, "I believe with perfect faith," and again he stopped. This happened a few times. Finally, R' Noach went over to him and asked him why he kept stopping.

"Rebbe," explained the chassid, "I recite the first few words, and then I think to myself, 'If I really believed with perfect faith, how could I ever commit a sin? And since I do sin, that must mean that I don't believe with perfect faith. How, then, can I recite the rest of the text? It's as if I were lying."

"This should be understood," said R' Noach, "as a prayer: I pray to believe with perfect faith, so that I will not sin in the future."

◄§ Keeping His Word

R' Nachum of Chernobyl found out that a certain small village did not have a *mikveh*. Contacting a wealthy man, R' Nachum offered to sell the man his entire portion in the World-to-Come if the man paid to have a *mikveh* built. The man jumped at the opportunity. They immediately sat down and drafted an agreement to this effect, which both signed.

Later, R' Nachum's chassidim asked him why he had gone so far to have the *mikveh* built. "Twice a day," said R' Nachum, "when we recite the *Shema*, we say that we must love Hashem *bechol me'odecha*, which means with all our wealth. I have nothing of any monetary value, except perhaps my share in the World-to-Come. If that's the only thing that I have for which anyone would pay money, I have to sell it in order to serve Hashem *bechol me'odecha*. If I didn't do so, I would be lying each time I recited the *Shema*."

◄§ Learning From a Non-Jew

R' Simchah Bunim of Pshischa once said, "When I was a young man, I learned a valuable lesson from a non-Jew in how to serve Hashem. I came across a non-Jewish wagon driver whose wagon was stuck in the mud. He asked me to help him push the wagon out of the mud, but I told him that I was too weak. 'You're not too weak,' he said to me. 'You're too lazy.' From him I learned that 'weakness' is often no more than laziness."

Torah Study

◄§ *Another Good Idea*

R' Chaim Brisker once attended a gathering of rabbis, where, under pressure from the Czarist government, a resolution was passed that every rabbi must know Russian. Immediately after the resolution was passed, R' Chaim took the floor with a resolution of his own. "I propose," he said, "a resolution that every rabbi must know *Shas* and *poskim*."

◄§ *At Least We're Sure of That*

A young man applied to learn in the yeshiva of the *Sha'agas Aryeh*. The *Sha'agas Aryeh* tested him, and found him to be totally ignorant. "In which yeshiva did you eat until now?" asked the *Sh'agas Aryeh*.

"Rebbe, don't you mean where did I learn?" asked the young man.

"No, I meant exactly what I said," responded the *Sha'agas Aryeh*. "That you ate I am sure; that you learned I'm not so sure."

Children Learn From Their Parents

A chassid told R' Menachem Mendel of Kotzk that he wanted his sons to study Torah regularly. "If your children see you studying Torah regularly," said R' Menachem Mendel, "they too will study Torah regularly. Otherwise, they will grow up to be adults who want their children to study Torah regularly, without doing so themselves."

A Cure for Forgetfulness

A chassid complained to R' Avraham Abush of Frankfurt that he had a terrible memory and forgot whatever he learned. "The cure," said R' Avraham Abush, "is to do *teshuvah*. We are told that *teshuvah* reaches Hashem's *Kisei Hakavod* — his Throne of Glory and in our prayers on Rosh Hashanah we say that 'there is no forgetfulness before Your *Kisei Hakavod*.' "

Another Cure

A chassid complained of his poor memory to the *Chiddushei HaRim*. "The cure for that," said the *Chiddushei HaRim*, "is stated in two verses in the Torah: 'do not be led astray by your heart and your eyes ... that you may remember.' "

A Hundred and One Times

We are told in the *Gemara* that a person who studies a passage of *Gemara* a hundred times is not the same as one who studies the same passage a hundred and one times. R'

Reuven Leib Himelstein deliberately studied a specific passage one hundred and one times, yet it was one with which he always had trouble in later years. Finally, he sat down and analyzed the situation. "The *Gemara* passage which gives the difference between a hundred and a hundred and one times," he explained, "does not refer to a person who simply reads a passage over by rote time after time. In such a case, there is indeed no real difference between a hundred times and a hundred and one times. What the *Gemara* is referring to is a person who picks up a passage of the *Gemara* and each time studies it anew, as if he had never seen it before. This way, indeed, a person who studies a passage the hundred and first time may notice something in it that he had never noticed before, and such a person is different from the one who has only studied the passage a hundred times."

⮤ *For Your Benefit*

A chassid once asked the author of *Chiddushei HaRim* whether he should seek a career as a *sofer*, writing Torah scrolls, *tefillin,* and *mezuzos*, or become a teacher of Torah. "You should definitely become a teacher," replied the *Chiddushei HaRim*. "One day you may come across an exceptional student, and then you, too, will learn."

⮤ *How Not to Fear the Darkness*

A chassid once asked R' Yisrael of Ruzhin, "Rebbe, whenever I study *Gemara*, I feel light within myself. However, as soon as I stop, the darkness envelops me. Why is that?"

"Let me give you an analogy," said R' Yisrael. "Imagine a man walking in the deepest forest in the middle of a dark night. He is accompanied by another man who is carrying a lantern. As long as the two walk together, the first man has light. But, if they come to a parting of the ways, the man without the lantern is plunged into darkness. If a man has light of his own, he need never fear the darkness."

ᴥ Learning a Lesson

The *Yehudi Hakadosh* said, "I learned diligence in my Torah studies from a blacksmith. I would see this man working from early in the morning until late in the evening, and always remaining cheerful as he worked. I thought to myself, 'Should I be less diligent in my Torah study, which feeds the spirit, than he is in his work, which only feeds the body?' "

ᴥ Never Be Satisfied

Once, after a *shiur*, the *Chiddushei HaRim* saw some of his students sitting back contentedly. He commented, "Anyone satisfied with what he knows, knows nothing. *Chazal* tell us with respect to money that a person who has any given quantity of money will want more. Only a person who has nothing doesn't want more than he already has."

ᴥ No Reason to Be Lonely

A Jew who lived in an isolated village complained to R' Dov Ber of Radoshitz that he was very lonely. R' Dov Ber asked him, "How can you be lonely when you can be friends with Abaye and Rava? They're the best possible companions."

ᴥ Talmud, Torah

R' Chaim of Volozhin had the custom of taking a Torah scroll out of the Ark just before *Kol Nidrei*, and while holding it, addressing his students.

Even in the very last year of his life, when he was very frail, he refused to change this practice. With the assistance of two students supporting him on either side, he went up to the Ark, took out a Torah scroll and said: "Our teacher, Moshe, it was you who received the Torah from Sinai. I want you to know that without our *Gemara*, there would not have been much value to your Torah. Indeed, those who denied the

Gemara were soon lost to the Jewish fold. It was the *Gemara* which prevented the Torah from being forgotten."

Turning to the yeshiva students, he continued, "My dear students, you must devote all your time to studying the *Gemara*, because that is what has ensured our survival all these years and has made our Torah an eternal one."

⋅⋗ The Answer Is in Keeping With the Question

When R' Levi Yitzchak of Berdichev received a copy of the *Shulchan Aruch HaRav* by the *Baal HaTanya*, he was totally overwhelmed by the tremendous scholarship of the author. R' Levi Yitzchak was concerned, however, that this phenomenal brilliance and erudition might lead the *Baal HaTanya* to conceit, and devised a scheme to prevent this.

R' Levi Yitzchak concocted an extremely difficult question in *halachah* and sent it to the *Baal HaTanya*. The *Baal HaTanya* wrestled with the question and weighed both sides back and forth. His inability to reach a conclusion shook his confidence.

When R' Levi Yitzchak met the *Baal HaTanya*, he told him that the case was entirely made up and that its entire purpose had been to ensure that he did not become conceited.

"Now I understand why I had such difficulty answering the question," said the *Baal HaTanya*. "In various places, *Chazal* tell us that a true decision must be reached 'to its truth.' Now that seems superfluous. If a decision is true, what does 'to its truth' mean? This means," he explained, "that a decision can only be true if the question was a true one. On the other hand, if the question is untrue, then the answer cannot be true."

⋅⋗ The Purpose

The *Chafetz Chaim* once remarked, "I don't understand why people question those who spend their time learning Torah and ask them what the *tachlis* (purpose) is. We are told in *Pirkei Avos* , 'If you have learned much Torah, don't become conceited, for that is the reason you were created.' Thus we see that the entire *tachlis* of life is to study Torah. Why then do people ask about the *tachlis* of the *tachlis*?"

∽§ *The Quarter Hour*

A *talmid chacham* studied a particularly difficult topic in the *Gemara* for two weeks, and even then was still left with very difficult questions. He called R' Moshe Feinstein and explained the problem he was having understanding the topic. "Please call me back in fifteen minutes," said R' Moshe.

A quarter of an hour later, the young man called again, and R' Moshe gave him a thorough explanation of all the points which had been troubling him. Reflecting later on their exchange, the young man commented, "Had Reb Moshe answered immediately, I would have been impressed by the depth of his answer, but I would have assumed that he had just studied the topic. When he asked me to call him back fifteen minutes later, I realized that he used that time to review the entire topic again. My amazement at his clarity after such a short review knows no bounds."

∽§ *To Remain an Am HaAretz*

Throughout his life, R' Moshe Feinstein spent every spare minute, beginning from four o'clock in the morning, learning. When he was eighty-five and staying in a bungalow for the summer, his wife tried to persuade him to rise a little later each day, so that he could enjoy some much-needed rest. "If I don't get up then," he replied, "I'll remain an *am ha'aretz* — an ignoramus."

∽§ *To Whom to Attribute Success*

R' Yechiel Michel of Zlotchov used to say: "If a person engages in business without studying Torah, he'll think that his success is due to his own abilities. But once a person begins to study Torah, he realizes that he cannot attribute his success to himself. The Torah teaches him to whom the success is really attributable."

⋖ Where Does a Fortress Belong?

The *Chiddushei HaRim* did not build his home and *beis medrash* in Warsaw proper, but in an outlying suburb, in which very few Jews lived.

The Rav of Warsaw, R' Dov Ber Meisels, came to visit the completed complex and asked the *Chiddushei HaRim* why he had chosen this location. Before the *Chiddushei HaRim* could answer, R' Dov Ber ventured his own explanation: "I assume that you intended to build a fortress to protect the Jews of Warsaw, and a fortress is built outside the city itself."

With a smile, the *Chiddushei HaRim* replied: "That was exactly what I had in mind."

⋖ Why Do You Sleep?

R' Shlomo of Radomsk once found one of the students asleep in the *beis medrash* when he should have been learning. R' Shlomo woke him and asked him, "Have you answered the question of the *rav ha'chovel* — the ship's captain?" Seeing that the student did not understand what he meant, R' Shlomo explained, "I'm referring to the question posed by the ship's captain to Yonah during the storm, 'Why are you asleep? Get up, and call to your God.' "

⋖ You've Got Your Priorities Wrong

A Jew went into business after years of studying in yeshiva. Some time later, he came to R' Meir of Premishlan and poured out his tale of woe. "Rebbe," he said, "I've gotten involved in a major business deal, and it just doesn't give me rest. All day I'm involved in it, and at night I stay up worrying about it. What should I do?"

"Well, if you're involved in this day and night," asked the Rebbe, "when do you have time to sit and learn Torah?"

"Unfortunately, Rebbe," replied the man, "I simply don't have time to study Torah. Once I've managed to conclude this deal, I'll be able to take time off to study Torah."

"You've got your priorities all wrong," said R' Meir. "The Torah tells us that if we keep the *mitzvos* of the Torah — and learning Torah is the most important — then we will receive a blessing from Hashem. You, however, are waiting for the blessing before you devote yourself to Torah. If you would just take the time to learn Torah, you'll soon find that your business problems will take care of themselves."

⋙ Comparisons

A yeshiva student was doing poorly in his learning, and the *roshei yeshiva* debated whether he should be allowed to remain. They brought the question to the *Chazon Ish*, who answered them sharply, "How do you know that he is not doing well? No doubt because there are other students who are doing better. If you remove him, however, there will be another student who is the weakest, and, according to your logic, you will then have to expel him as well. Eventually, you will have to expel all the students from the yeshiva."

⋙ Mazel Tov! Mazel Tov!

R' Chaim of Brisk always made fun of those who propounded outlandish *p'shatim* in their study of *Gemara* in order to show their brilliance. He once got into a discussion with a *rav* who suggested that the act of marriage might be viewed not as a single act of "acquisition" by the husband but as an ongoing series of "acquisition."

"In that case," said Reb Chaim, "let me be the first to offer you *mazel tov,* since according to that, you and your wife are getting married every second."

◂§ Seeing the Sounds

R' Azriel Hildesheimer of Berlin once came to Warsaw where he met with the first Gerrer Rebbe, the *Chiddushei HaRim.* They naturally began speaking in learning, and as it was *Parashas Yisro,* R' Azriel asked the *Chiddushei HaRim,* "What does it mean that the people 'saw the sounds'? What type of miracle was that?"

"In Hebrew," replied the *Chiddushei HaRim,* "there are many words which sound the same, although they are written differently and have different meanings. In the Ten Commandments, for instance, we are told, 'You shall not steal,' where the Hebrew for 'you shall not' is *lo,* spelled with an *alef* (לא). Now, imagine if people had heard and understood this as *lo* with a *vav* rather than an *alef* (לו), which means 'for him.' People might then understand the verse to mean, 'for Him (i.e., Hashem) you may steal.' Thus the Torah tells us that not only did the Jews *hear* the Torah, but they saw before their eyes what the correct meaning was."

◂§ In the Shadow of Death

A.L. Horowitz was one of a group of religious Jews assigned to a brush factory in a concentration camp. The prisoners were given a weekly quota, and rushed frantically throughout the week to fill their quotas by Friday. On Shabbos they only pretended to be working unless a guard came over.

The prisoners even arranged a *Gemara shiur* on Shabbos, using a small *Gemara* that had been smuggled into the camp. They would sit around the table, and the one at the head of the table would read from the *Gemara.* Each prisoner always kept a half-finished brush by him in case a guard ventured by.

R' Shmelke of Nikolsburg and his brother, R' Pinchas of Koretz, once came to the Gaon of Vilna and heard a brilliant Torah discourse from him. After he had finished, the brothers looked at each other. They had been steeped in the *pilpul* method, which introduces all types of complexities, and yet the Gaon's discourse had seemed so straightforward. They went over what they had heard and began to apply the *pilpul* method to the Gaon's Torah, adding layer upon layer of questions and answers drawn from sources all over *Shas*.

As they delved deeper and deeper, they were unaware that the Gaon was listening to them. As soon as they finished, the Gaon said, "I listened with great interest to your *pilpul*. Would you mind if I repeat it to you?" He then began to review everything they had said. Then to their great delight, the Gaon picked up from where they had left off, and, using the *pilpul* method, wove together the most beautiful Torah structure.

As they listened excitedly, they realized that the Gaon was reaching conclusions that were clearly against the *halachah*.

When the Gaon had finished, the brothers were speechless. How could it be that he had come to so many conclusions so clearly against indisputable laws of the *Shulchan Aruch*?

At that point, the Gaon turned to them and said, "I want you to realize that *pilpul* is a two-edged sword. One can come up with all types of dazzling conclusions, but one can also veer completely away from the *halachah*, without even realizing he is doing so. In fact, if one uses *pilpul* consistently, he can eventually come to believe that his thinking is so brilliant that he has the right to contradict the greatest Sages of the past. Only if a person studies the *Gemara* by delving into it deeply, laboring to understand exactly what the previous generations of great scholars said, will he realize how small are our intellects in comparison with theirs. We can spend hours understanding a certain idea, and then find it encapsulated in a few choice words of *Rashi* or another commentator."

◄§ *The Right Tractate to Study*

When the brothers R' Shmelke of Nikolsburg and R' Pinchas of Koretz were seven and five respectively, their father R' Zvi Hirsh of Chortkow learned all of *Gemara Pesachim* with them between Purim and Pesach. After they had completed the tractate, R' Zvi Hirsh asked his sons what tractate they wanted to learn next. Shmelke, the elder brother, answered that they should learn *Shevuos,* which at the rate of a folio a day they could complete in time for the Shavuos festival."

Their father smiled. "Shmelke, my son," asked R' Zvi Hirsh, "do you really think that the tractate deals with the festival of Shavuos?"

"No, father," replied Shmelke. "I know that *Shevuo*s deals with oaths (*shevuos*) that a person takes, and what the law is if he takes an oath in vain, etc. However, it was on the festival of Shavuos that we received the Torah and took an oath to obey the Torah. I think that we should study the tractate of *Shevuo*s right now, so that we will be able to truly appreciate the importance of the oath that we took at Mt. Sinai."

◄§ *Pride of a Mother*

R' Shmelke of Nikolsburg and his brother, R' Pinchas of Koretz, devoted all their time to Torah study from a very young age. R' Shmelke never ate bread so as not to have to take time from his studies to wash before the meal or to recite *Bircas Hamazon* afterwards. His brother, R' Pinchas, would stay up all night studying Torah. Their mother used to joke, "I have two sons. One of them never says the *Bircas Hamazon* and the other never recites the *Shema* when going to sleep at night."

⋐ That, Too, Is a Way to Serve Hashem

R' Shmelke of Nikolsburg employed all types of devices to minimize the amount of time he slept in order to have more time for Torah study. For instance, he never went to sleep in a bed but only while seated at a table.

R' Elimelech of Lizhensk once visited him and saw that he was utterly exhausted. R' Elimelech begged R' Shmelke to go to sleep in a bed, and R' Shmelke finally gave in. As soon as his head touched the pillow, he fell fast asleep. R' Elimelech covered him with a blanket, and he slept until dawn. After washing their hands and reciting the morning blessings, R' Shmelke and R' Elimelech sat down to study a difficult passage in the *Gemara*. R' Shmelke soon realized that his mind was clearer than it had been in many months. "I see," he said, "that by sleeping one can also serve Hashem."

High Holidays

✑ A Cause for Joy

On *erev* Yom Kippur, the Baal Shem Tov was seen striding joyfully down the street. A man stopped him and asked why he was so happy when everyone else was solemn with thoughts of the impending Day of Judgment. "After all," said the man, "if your verdict is negative, you certainly have no cause to rejoice. And if you are happy because you are convinced that your verdict will be favorable, isn't that conceit?"

"The verdict is entirely irrelevant to me," replied the Baal Shem Tov. "I am rejoicing because there is both a Judge and judgment in the world."

✑ A Remarkable Prayer

Two great Torah giants, the *Netziv* and R' Yitzchak Elchanan Spektor, were forced to travel to the Russian capital, St. Petersburg, to take care of an urgent matter affecting the Jewish population. They planned to return home for Yom Kippur, but were unable to complete their work in time.

On *Kol Nidrei* evening, they went to the only *shul* in walking distance. The *shul* was exclusively comprised of Cantonists — men who had been seized as children by the Czar's troops to serve in the Russian army for a period of twenty-five years. Only Jews who had served in the army were permitted to live in the capital. Naturally, these men knew very little, having spent most of their lives in remote areas of the Russian empire.

As they approached *Kol Nidrei*, an old Cantonist got up to address the men present, as follows: "My brothers, we all know that at this time Jews turn to Hashem and ask Him for three things: children, life, and sustenance. What should we pray for? Shall we pray for children? Of course not — we're not allowed to marry because we're in the army. Shall we pray for life? What worth is our lives anyway, when at any minute we may lose it in defending this country? Shall we pray for sustenance? We have all of our food supplied by the Czar. Thus, dear brothers, there isn't a thing we have to pray for ourselves. All that we can pray for is that *Yisgadal Veyiskadash shemei rabba* — May Hashem's great name be exalted and sanctified." At this, all broke into tears. It is said that the two *gedolim* counted this as the most outstanding Yom Kippur in their lives.

✑ Fasting Twice

The *Chazon Ish* visited a man who had been ordered by his doctors not to fast on Yom Kippur due to illness. "Ever since I was a child," the man lamented, "I have observed every fast, even the most minor, and now I have to eat on Yom Kippur."

"You are wrong," said the *Chazon Ish*. "In fact, you will have the reward of a double fast tomorrow. As you know, *Chazal* tell us that if one eats on the day before Yom Kippur, it is as if he fasted on both the ninth and the tenth of *Tishrei*. If you are required by your poor health to eat tomorrow, it will also be considered as if you have fasted for two days. We all must listen to the Word of Hashem. If He commands us to fast, we must fast, and if He commands us to eat, we must eat."

≈§ Give a Clear Answer!

The Rebbe of Rachmistrivka became gravely ill, and the doctor attending him decided that he had to eat on Yom Kippur.

Now came the hard part — how to tell the Rebbe about it. Entering the Rebbe's room, the doctor began stammering, "Rebbe, Rebbe — you see, based on what I found, well, you see, Yom Kippur is coming, and. . . ."

At that point the Rebbe cut him off. "What are you trying to tell me? That I'm not allowed to fast on Yom Kippur?"

"Yes," said the doctor, much relieved.

"Well, a decision like that must be stated clearly and without hesitation. You have to be completely decisive in such matters."

≈§ "Give Us at Least One Day"

R' Yaakov Meir Grodzenski of Bobroisk insisted one year that the prayer for the welfare of Czar, which was recited in every *shul* in Russia on Shabbos and festivals, would not be recited on Yom Kippur. "Give us at least one day a year," he would explain, "when we can accept fully the Yoke of Heaven, without having to accept the 'yoke' of flesh and blood."

～ In Its Season

"Everything has its season," said R' Yitzchak of Worka. "If one tries to sell something out of season, when there are few buyers, any buyer will haggle endlessly over the price, and no price will be low enough. On the other hand, when something is in season, the reverse is true. Buyers outbid one another and the price goes up and up.

"The Ten Days of Repentance," he concluded, "are a seller's market for *teshuvah*. During that time, any *teshuvah*, regardless of its quality, will be snapped up by Hashem. But we must be sure that we have 'merchandise' for sale."

～ It's Never Too Late

R' Yechiel Michel of Gustinin once entreated his *shamash* on the day before Yom Kippur, "Feivel, let us both do *teshuvah*. It's not too late. Part of a day is *halachically* considered to be like the whole day, and even a single day is considered like the entire year. Thus if we do *teshuvah* now, it will be as if we had done *teshuvah* throughout the entire year."

～ It's What Happens Between That Counts

A noted *chazan* always burst into tears at the words, "Man is created from dust and his end is dust," in the *U'nesaneh tokef* prayer of Rosh Hashanah. A chassid approached him after *davening* one year and said, "Why were you crying? Had it been said, 'Man is created from gold and his end is dust,' I might have understood your weeping. But since man was created from dust and returns to dust, what has he lost? On the contrary, between being created from dust and returning to dust, man has the opportunity to do so much in the interim — to perform another *mitzvah*, to do another good deed, and so on."

◄§ Listening to Hashem

The *Chiddushei HaRim* once went to visit a sick man on Yom Kippur. The man was despondent because he had been required to eat on Yom Kippur. "I see no reason for you to be upset," said the *Chiddushei HaRim.* "The same One Who ordered us to fast on Yom Kippur ordered you to eat."

◄§ Planning for the Future

Prior to Yom Kippur, R' Yisrael Salanter would place a number of cookies in his *shtender.* He wanted to be sure to have food immediately at hand if a question of danger to a person's life arose.

◄§ When to Begin

R' Yisrael Salanter used to say: "Many people prepare themselves for repentance during the Ten Days of Repentance. The more scrupulous begin from the beginning of *Elul.* I say, however, that one must begin to repent immediately after *Ne'ilah* the preceding Yom Kippur."

◄§ With Lavan I Have Lived

R' Chaim of Sanz once rose before the Rosh Hashanah *davening* to address his chassidim. As was customary, he had his *tallis* over his head. As he stood there, he lifted his white beard and exclaimed, quoting our father Yaakov in *Bereishis* 32:5: "'With Lavan I lived' — I have lived all this time until my beard turned white (*lavan*), and yet 'I have delayed until now' — I have still not repented properly." He immediately burst into tears, and all his chassidim began crying bitterly.

⊷§ A Higher Level of Prayer

A prominent Jewish professor once visited R' Aryeh Levin the day before Yom Kippur. He confessed that he was bothered that he felt no differently than usual despite the onset of Yom Kippur. R' Aryeh jumped up, clutched the professor's hands in his own, and told him, "I envy you. You worry about not being able to pray, whereas all my prayers are by rote. With your sensitivity, I am convinced that you will indeed pray properly tomorrow."

⊷§ A Lesson to Hashem

R' Elimelech of Lizhensk was known for defending the Jewish people before Hashem. One Rosh Hashanah, before the blowing of the *shofar*, he made an impassioned appeal: "Hashem, in the *piyut* we say, 'He who acquired His servants in judgment; He who has mercy on His people in judgment.' Hashem, permit me, Elimelech ben Eliezer Lipa, to remind You, with trembling, of the *Gemara* (*Kiddushin* 20a). Whoever acquires a Jewish servant acquires a master for himself, because the master has to ensure his servant's welfare in accordance with the verse (*Devarim* 15:16), 'for it is good for him with you.' This means the master has to feed his slave properly. Since we are Your servants, as it states in the Torah (*Vayikra* 25:42), 'for they are My slaves,' You are required to have mercy on Your nation on this Day of Judgment and to see to the provisions of Your people throughout the coming year."

⊷§ Not a Single Deliberate Sinner

R' Levi Yitzchak of Berdichev once addressed Hashem before Yom Kippur as follows:

"Hashem, in the prayer before *Kol Nidrei*, we state, 'Let us forgive the entire community of the Children of Israel, because all have sinned through negligence.' What does that mean, then: no one committed a sin deliberately? The answer is exactly that — every single sin a Jew commits is done through negligence rather than deliberately. The proof of this is simple: Has a Jew ever recited the *leshem yichud* entreaty (recited by many before performing a *mitzvah*) before committing a sin?"

⊷ Public versus Private Domain

R' Yisrael Salanter was walking down the street the day before Yom Kippur when he met another Jew. R' Yisrael asked the man how he was, and the man started crying hysterically. After R' Yisrael had calmed him down somewhat, he asked the man what was bothering him so greatly. "Rebbe," the man said, "I'm terrified of the judgment against me on Yom Kippur."

Seeing that the man's actions were affecting other people in the street as well, R' Yisrael said to him, "Your heart is a private domain. In your heart, you may cry as much as you wish. Your face, on the other hand, is a public domain, and you don't have the right to burden others with your personal problems."

⊷ Credit Only Where It Is Due

The Dubno *Maggid* once found himself in a certain city for Rosh Hashanah, and was naturally asked to speak. Before speaking he was told that many of the congregants attended *shul* only three days a year. That information suggested to him the following parable:

A storekeeper had a fire in his small shop, which destroyed everything he owned. Even worse, all the goods in the store had been taken on credit. The unfortunate storekeeper was not only without money or merchandise, he owed thousands of rubles for the goods.

As the time drew closer for his debt to be paid, he became more and more distraught. What could he do? Finally, he decided to go to the wholesaler from whom he had acquired the goods and beg him for an extension of time. Otherwise, he would be lost.

As he approached the wholesaler's home, he became more and more frightened. How would the man act? Would he have him thrown in prison? And then what would become of the storekeeper's family?

He came to the wholesaler's door, but couldn't bring himself to knock. He just stood there unable to move and finally began crying uncontrollably. Hearing the noise, the wholesaler came out. "My dear fellow," he said, "what is the problem? We've been working together for so many years. Surely I can help you. Meanwhile, come in and we'll see what we can do."

Finally, after a glass of tea had been brought, the storekeeper was able to control himself enough to be able to tell his story between sobs. "I-I-I've had a fire. It destroyed everything I owned, as well as everything you gave me on credit. I have no way of repaying you."

The wholesaler was very moved by the tale. "Don't worry," he said, "after all of the years we've worked together and the profit I've made from working with you, I'll forgive this debt. Furthermore, in order to get you back on your feet again, I'll send you a new load of goods on credit."

Overjoyed, the storekeeper returned home.

Word of what had happened soon spread. Another storekeeper, who heard of the wholesaler's generosity, decided that he would see what he could get from the wholesaler. He stood outside the wholesaler's door and sobbed away. When the wholesaler opened the door and asked him what he wanted, he asked for two thousand rubles. "Why should I give it to you?" asked the wholesaler.

"But your excellency, you gave my fellow storekeeper thousands of rubles," the man stuttered.

"How dare you think that I'd give you thousands of rubles just like that, you fool! What *chutzpah*! The storekeeper is someone I've been working with for many years. I know him and I trust him. He and I have both benefited from our business together. But why should I help you?"

"The moral," concluded the Dubno *Maggid,* "is that if a Jew comes to *shul* regularly throughout the year, if he has 'dealings' with Hashem 365 days a year and tries to fulfill the *mitzvos* even if he sins here and there, he can come to Hashem and ask Him to forgive this sin or that. But if a Jew comes to *shul* only during the *Yamim Nora'im,* without having any dealings with Hashem throughout the year, and asks for the priceless gift of good health and for sustenance in the coming year, his request is deemed nothing but *chutzpah.*"

⋖ *Why Did You Wait Until Now?*

R' Aharon of Karlin was once the *chazan* for *Shacharis* on Rosh Hashanah. However, as soon as he recited the very first word, *HaMelech* (the King), he burst into bitter tears and was unable to continue. Later, his chassidim asked him: "Rebbe, what caused you to break down crying the way you did?"

He explained, "No sooner did I say the word *HaMelech* than I was reminded of a story in the *Gemara.* When R' Yochanan ben Zakkai came to Vespasian, he greeted Vespasian with the words, 'Peace be to you, O king, peace be to you, O king.' When Vespasian, who had not yet received news of his appointment by the Roman Senate, heard this, he replied: 'You deserve death for one of two reasons: If I am not the king, how dare you refer to me that way? And if I am the king, why did you not come to me until now?'

"Therefore," said R' Aharon, "when I referred to Hashem as *HaMelech,* I was filled with remorse. As Hashem is the King, why have I not come to Him in repentance until now?"

⋖ *A Fruitless Search*

Just before *Kol Nidrei* one Yom Kippur, R' Levi Yitzchak of Berdichev took a candle and started searching underneath the benches. "What are you looking for, Rebbe?" the people asked."

"I'm looking for a drunk, but there isn't a single one in sight," said R' Levi Yitzchak.

Then, as was his practice, he began addressing Hashem:

"Lord of the Universe!" he said, "See how great Your people, Israel, are. You gave us a *mitzvah* to eat and drink on the day before Yom Kippur, and You even stated that to eat and drink on that day is as great as fasting on *Yom Kippur*. Now, had you given such a *mitzvah* to the non-Jews, how many of them would have been rolling around in the gutter drunk? How many of them would have been involved in fights and come out bruised? Yet, in spite of the *mitzvah* to eat and drink, here you find all of Israel gathering early in *shul* in anticipation of Yom Kippur. Lord of the Universe! Isn't the merit of that alone enough for You to forgive them for all their sins?"

Holidays

⋖ *Decorating the Sukkah*

It was customary among Galician Jews to decorate their *sukkos* lavishly. They even imported *sukkah* decorations from abroad.

R' Chaim of Sanz was vehemently opposed to the practice. "They are all violating the rule against being wasteful (*baal tashchis*)," he said. The Sanzer Rebbe limited himself to a few simple decorations and used the money left him by his chassidim for the poor instead.

"The best *sukkah* decoration," he would say, "is to ensure that the poor do not go hungry during the festival."

✺ The Other Four

A chassid asked R' Eliezer of Dzikov for a *berachah* that he obtain a fine set of the Four Species.

"More important," said R' Eliezer, "are the four attributes: kindness of the heart, humility of the spirit, truthfulness of the mind, and the desire to improve yourself."

✺ The Hardest Mitzvah

R' Eliyahu, the Gaon of Vilna, was once asked what is the hardest *mitzvah* to perform. The Gaon replied that he had examined all the *mitzvos*, and that the hardest one to perform is undoubtedly the *mitzvah* of rejoicing during Sukkos. The Torah specifies that one must rejoice every moment of the seven days and nights of the festival. That entire time a person is forbidden to have any sad thoughts whatsoever. "That," he said, "is indeed the most difficult *mitzvah*."

✺ The Choice

R' Chaim of Brisk once had two *esrogim* brought to him for Sukkos. One *esrog* came from *Eretz Yisrael,* but was not particularly attractive. On the other hand, it was undoubtedly kosher. The second *esrog* was from Corfu and was the exact opposite of the first: It was extremely attractive, but there were doubts as to whether it was from a "grafted" species, which might invalidate it. R' Chaim decided to use both, one after the other. One might have assumed that he would use the *Eretz Yisrael esrog* first because that was definitely kosher. R' Chaim, however, chose to use the Corfu *esrog* first. He explained as follows:

"Let's say I use the *Eretz Yisrael esrog* first. There is no doubt that I have fulfilled the *mitzvah* since the *esrog* is definitely kosher. If I then take the Corfu *esrog*, I have done nothing, for I have already fulfilled the *mitzvah* with an unattractive *esrog*. On the other hand, if I take the Corfu *esrog* first, if it is kosher, I will have fulfilled the *mitzvah* with an attractive *esrog*. On the other hand, if it is not kosher, at least I will fulfill the *mitzvah* afterwards with the kosher *Eretz Yisrael esrog*."

ᴇᔆ Mixed Sentiments

Once, on Simchas Torah, when all were dancing joyfully with the Torah, the *talmidim* of R' Yisrael Salanter noticed that he looked sad and asked him why. "Imagine," said R' Yisrael, "that a man is sad about one event and happy about another. In such a case, the joy may overcome the sadness. What happens, however, if the joy and the sadness come from the same source?

"Imagine, for example, if a man has a son whom he loves very dearly, and that son becomes extremely ill. Can the joy of having such a son outweigh the sadness of the fact that he is sick? Of course not. On the contrary, the more the father loves his son, the more he will feel sad over his son's illness.

"It's the same with me. On the one hand, I rejoice greatly in the fact that we have the precious Torah. On the other hand, I am terribly saddened that there are so many Jews who violate the Torah daily. Thus, the more joy there is on Simchas Torah, the more keenly I feel pain over the level to which we have sunk in our observance."

ᴇᔆ The Logic Is Inverted

The *Chiddushei HaRim* used to say, "A common misconception is that on Simchas Torah we celebrate the completion of the Torah reading. That's wrong. On Simchas Torah, we celebrate beginning the Torah reading all over."

ᴇᔆ What Piety!

In R' Yonasan Eybeschuetz's *shul*, a very wealthy man bought the privilege of *Chasan Torah* on Simchas Torah and insisted on keeping the honor for himself, despite being a total ignoramus in Torah studies. R' Yonasan commented archly, "The man is indeed extremely pious. Imagine, he is a *chasan*, and he hasn't seen the *kallah* for the entire past year!"

✍§ Mutuality

A *rav* once observed a totally unlearned Jew dancing with great abandon and joy with a *sefer Torah* on Simchas Torah and questioned the man as to why he was so filled with joy. "I study Torah all year," said the *rav*, "and thus I am filled with great joy, but why are you so happy?"

"Rabbi," answered the man, "on Yom Kippur, when we recite the *vidui* — confession — we ask forgiveness for 'the sin which we sinned with taking bribes.' When would a simple workingman like myself ever have the chance to be guilty of taking a bribe? Nevertheless, I still seek forgiveness for this sin, because 'all Jews are guarantors for one another.' If I can be partners with you in your sins, can I not also be partners with you in your Torah study?"

✍§ It's the Same Hashem

On a Friday afternoon during Chanukah, R' Shmuel of Slonim made his preparations for lighting the Chanukah candles. He then went over to see his grandfather, the *Yesod HaAvodah*, light his menorah, allowing himself barely enough time to return and kindle his own Chanukah lights. While he was away, one of the many visitors in his house, seeing the Chanukah lights prepared, lit them himself.

When R' Shmuel returned home, he saw the lights burning and realized that there was no time to prepare another set. "The same Hashem who commanded us to kindle the Chanukah lights also commanded us not to become angry," he said to himself, and he went to *shul* to welcome Shabbos cheerfully.

✦ One Must Rejoice

The Jews in the Warsaw Ghetto, starving, beaten, threatened with death at any moment, found it exceptionally difficult to observe the festival day of Purim. R' Klonymos of Pischena, a chassidic *rebbe*, told them, "The *Zohar* states that *Yom Kippurim* — Yom Kippur — must be a day 'like Purim.' Thus, just as on Yom Kippur one must fast whether he wants to or not, on Purim one must rejoice whether he wants to or not — even if the devil himself surrounds us."

✦ Haman Is Easier

Students of the Novarodok yeshiva led by R' Yozl Horowitz, put on a Purim play one year, in which students portrayed Mordechai and Haman. Later, R' Yozl remarked, "It's much easier to play the part of Haman, because each of us has within himself something of Haman's conceit. To play the part of Mordechai, however, is much more difficult."

✦ The Difference

"The difference between Yom Kippur and Purim," said R' Levi Yitzchak of Berdichev, "is that on Yom Kippur we afflict our bodies by fasting, while on Purim we afflict our souls by drinking until one does not know the difference between 'Blessed be Mordechai' and 'Cursed be Haman.' Can there be any greater affliction than losing one's power of discernment?"

✦ Tzedakah Money

A simple, good-hearted man came to R' Noach of Lechevich on the day after Purim, very distraught. "Rebbe," he said, "we are told that on Purim one must distribute money to the poor. This morning, however, I was in the market square. I saw that a peasant had just brought in a tremendous load of firewood, and many Jews were buying firewood from him. Rebbe, where did they get the money if they gave away their money yesterday?"

"It's really simple," said R' Noach. "No doubt the people you saw buying firewood today were the ones to whom everyone else distributed *tzedakah* yesterday."

⋙ The One Depends on the Other

One year, R' Zvi Hirsh Berlin, the *rav* of Mannheim, did not give a sermon on *Shabbos HaGadol*, the Shabbos before Pesach. Some of the members of the community asked him why he had not followed the custom of giving a sermon on *Shabbos HaGadol*.

"*Chazal* tell us," R' Tzvi Hirsh answered, "that 'one asks and gives *derashos* on the laws of Pesach before Pesach.' Now what is meant by 'one asks and gives *derashos*?' The implication is that where people come to ask the *rav* questions about the laws of the festival, the *rav* gives a sermon to clarify various issues. Here no one comes to ask any questions in *halachah* — apparently everyone knows everything — and thus I am exempted from the obligation of giving sermons."

⋙ Biblical Proof

In Koenigsberg, Jewish residents were required to contribute to the Pesach *ma'os chittim* fund for the poor. A Russian Jew, who lived in Koenigsberg most of the year because of his business, refused to contribute. He claimed that because his wife and children were still in Russia he should not be considered a local resident.

When the community heads saw they were getting nowhere, they summoned the man to a *din Torah* — a Torah hearing — before the *Malbim*, who was then the *rav* of Koenigsberg. The *Malbim* refused to hear the case until the man agreed to abide by whatever decision was reached. The man agreed, but with one stipulation of his own: Since he was one of the *maskilim* — freethinkers — he refused to accept any proof from the Talmud. He would only accept proofs from *Tanach*.

"That's easy," said the *Malbim*. "In *Shmuel* we are told that Naval lived in Maon, but his work was in Carmel. A few chapters later, his wife Avigail is referred to as the wife of Naval the Carmelite. If Naval lived in Maon, why is he called the Carmelite? This shows that a person is considered to be a resident of the place where he works."

ᵂᵇ *Please Don't Make Me a Liar*

The community leaders of Radin once came to the *Chafetz Chaim* and complained that the contributions to the *ma'os chittim* fund for the poor at Pesach were inadequate. The *Chafetz Chaim* agreed to their request that he address the town's Jews.

When everyone had gathered in the *shul*, the *Chafetz Chaim* got up and said: "As you all know, I'm a very old man, and will soon be called to the other world — the World of Truth. There I will have to give a full accounting. When I am asked about the people of Radin, they will want to know everything about Radin, including how the people of Radin gave to the *ma'os chittim* campaign. I will then be faced with a dilemma. If I state that the people gave generously, it would be a lie, and I have never told a lie in my life. On the other hand, if I say that the people of Radin were not generous, that would be *lashon hara*, something of which I have also never been guilty. There is only one solution to my dilemma — for you to give generously to the *ma'os chittim* fund. That way I will be able to report with complete truth that the people of Radin did indeed support the *ma'os chittim* fund fully."

ᵂᵇ *Change of Occupation*

The day before Pesach, R' Avraham Yitzchak Kook's house would swarm with all types of people coming to visit him, making it difficult for his wife to prepare for the *Seder*. She complained to her husband, and he consoled her: "Imagine, Raize Rivkah, that I were a wine merchant. Wouldn't you be thrilled by the large number of people coming to our home to buy wine just before Pesach? Aren't you happier that I'm a *rav* and not a wine merchant?"

⋅ৡ A Bad Year

One year, very little rain fell in Lithuania and the price of wheat rose sharply. As a result, the *gabbaim* decided to cut the Pesach allocations of the poor.

When the Vilna Gaon heard of their decision, he told the *gabbaim*, "When the Torah commands us to eat *matzah*, it writes the word *matzos* without the letter *vav*, but when it states that '*matzos* shall be eaten,' the word *matzos* as a general rule has a *vav*. That teaches us that we may decrease the amount of *matzah* we ourselves eat, but we are not allowed to decrease the amount of *matzos* we give to the poor."

⋅ৡ The Real Reason

The *Avnei Nezer* would not permit his chassidim to join his *Seder*, no matter how much they implored him. The more brazen asked the Rebbe the reason for his refusal. They assumed that he must see Eliyahu in person during the *Seder*, and that was why he was so adamant.

"Not at all," replied the *Avnei Nezer*. "During the *Seder*, every man must feel that he is totally free. If a chassid joins his Rebbe's *Seder*, there is no way he can feel truly free."

⋅ৡ Big Deal!

R' Aharon of Chernobyl once addressed Hashem on Shavuos, the day on which the Torah was given. "Hashem," he said, "it is not surprising that the Jews in the desert accepted the Torah. After all, they were very wealthy, having received their wealth from the Egyptians. And they were in perfect health: As the *Midrash* tells us, all illness and physical infirmity were removed by You at Sinai. They were also free men. Thus, the conditions were ideal for them to accept the Torah.

"Today, the reverse is true. We are destitute. Our bodies are racked with pain. And we are subject to all the cruelty of a regime bent on destroying us as a people. Yet, I swear to You, that if You come to us today and offer us the Torah, we would all accept it with the same enthusiasm as did the Jews in the desert and we would observe it fully."

ᴈ§ *The True Test Comes Later*

The day after Shavuos, R' Simchah Bunim of Pshischa gathered together all the young men who learned with him and told them: "Immediately after the Torah was given, Hashem said to Moshe, 'Tell them, "Return to your tents." It is true that they have received the Torah, but now I want to see how they apply it in their daily lives.' The true test of receiving the Torah is what one does with the Torah he has received."

ᴈ§ *Advance Notice*

As he bade farewell to one of his chassidim after the Shavuos holiday, R' Simchah Bunim of Pshischa said, "Remember that we will soon be blowing the *shofar*."

ᴈ§ *Napoleon and Tishah B'Av*

In 1812, Napoleon's armies invaded Poland. As they were passing through a Jewish village, Napoleon heard the sound of a large number of people weeping. He sent one of his men to investigate to see if he could help.

As the soldier entered the building from which the wailing was emanating, he realized that he had entered a *shul*, and that everyone was sitting on the ground. After consulting with the elders, he found out that it was *Tishah B'Av*, and that they were mourning the destruction of the Temple in Jerusalem.

When he came back to Napoleon, the soldier reported, "Your excellency, these are Jews. There was a major calamity, and their synagogue was destroyed."

"Recently?" asked Napoleon.

"No, it occurred over 1700 years ago."

"Here?"

"No, your excellency, in Jerusalem."

"Remarkable," said Napoleon. "They are mourning for something that happened so long ago and so far away. Now I understand how the Jews have survived. A nation with memories that ancient, which still longs for deliverance after all these years, will continue to exist forever."

Sin and Repentance

ᴥ Looking for Adam

When R' Yechiel, the grandson of R' Baruch of Medzhibozh, was a young child he asked his grandfather, "If Hashem knows everything, why did He call out to Adam after his sin and say, 'Where are you?' " R' Baruch listened, but did not answer.

Some time later, R' Baruch asked the little Yechiel, "Would you like to play hide-and-seek?" The little boy was delighted and ran away to hide. He waited and waited, but his grandfather didn't come to look for him. Finally, he gave up and left his hiding place. His grandfather, he saw, was sitting at his desk, and had not even tried to look for him. Little

Yechiel burst into tears. "Grandfather, you forgot all about me! You never even tried to look for me!" he wailed.

"This," said R' Baruch, "is the answer to your question. Of course Hashem knew where Adam was. Adam, however, had committed two sins: by eating the fruit of the tree and by trying to hide from Hashem. Had Hashem not gone to 'look' for Adam, he would not have been able to survive because of his shame. By 'looking' for Adam, Hashem gave him the opportunity to again make contact with Him, so that he could once more face his Creator."

⮑ One Must Repent

The Shpoler Zayde was once very perturbed during his *tisch* on Friday night. "I am afraid," he told his chassidim, "that I might have accidentally lit a candle after the permitted time." All his chassidim began to assure him that it could not be so. After all, one argued, if Hashem does not permit the animals of *tzaddikim* to do anything wrong, then He surely wouldn't allow the *tzaddik* himself to err.

Only one chassid, R' Rafael of Barshad, disagreed. "It is indeed possible that the Rebbe might have erred accidentally," he said, "and he must do *teshuvah*."

The Shpoler Zayde turned to the chassidim and said, "Only R' Rafael is wise. Had it not been for him, I might not have repented, and died with my sin unatoned."

⮑ One Step at a Time

R' Yisrael Zalman of Sharshov, a disciple of R' Avraham of Slonim, once cried to R' Avraham, "Rebbe, all my life I have worked so hard to do *teshuvah*, and yet I don't see the slightest change in my character. What can I do?"

R' Avraham replied, "Imagine a man who is stuck in thick mud to his ankles. Each step he takes, he sinks again into the mud. He may think he is accomplishing nothing by taking these steps, but the truth is every single step brings him closer to dry land."

✥ The Sin Has Been Forgiven

R' Simchah Bunim of Pshischa was once sitting with his chassidim when he asked, "How do we know that a sin has been forgiven?" All the chassidim ventured different answers, but none satisfied R' Simchah Bunim. Finally he answered the question himself. "A sin has been forgiven," he said, "when one no longer repeats it."

✥ R' Zushia the "Sinner"

When R' Zushia of Hanipol saw a person sinning, he would never rebuke him. Instead, he would wait until the person was near him and begin crying to himself, "Zushia, how could you have committed such and such sin? Zushia, don't you realize that you will have to give an accounting for your actions in the World-to-Come? Woe is to you, Zushia!" He would repeat this numerous times, crying bitterly, until the other person realized the gravity of his sin and repented.

✥ Measuring Repentance

A man came to the Belzer Rebbe, R' Yisachar Dov, and told him, "Rebbe, I'm getting on in years, and I want to make sure that all my youthful sins have been forgiven. I have no idea what is considered repentance."

"Let me tell you a story," said R' Yisachar Dov. "A merchant brought some fabric which was in great demand to the fair. As soon as he arrived, it began raining without cessation. No other merchant was able to reach the fair at all. All the customers rushed to him to buy his wares, but he held off selling. By the next day, the amount offered for his fabric had risen dramatically, and the following day, it went up again. But still the merchant refused to sell, hoping that the longer he waited the higher the price would rise.

"Finally, the merchant decided to sell his fabric the next day. That night, however, the rain stopped, and by the next morning other merchants with the same fabric had arrived at the fair. The price of the fabric plummeted.

"If your regret over the sins in your youth is as great as that merchant's, you have repented sufficiently," said the Belzer.

◄§ The Proper Way to Fast

R' Yosef of Ostraha was against fasting on days other than those decreed by our Sages. He explained with an apt analogy. "Often," he said, "when a community wishes to impose a communal tax, it is structured so that the heaviest burden falls on the poor. When the tax collector comes to a poor man, he does not have enough money to pay. What does he do? He takes whatever little money he has and bribes the tax collector to leave him alone. But he still owes the same tax as before.

"The same is true of fasts. The 'rich' organs — the eyes, ears, and mouth — sin, but it is the stomach, which did not sin, that suffers. Meanwhile, the sins of the 'rich' organs remain unrepented.

"Better," R' Yosef concluded, "that the 'rich' organs repent — the mouth stop speaking slander and falsehood, the eyes not see what is forbidden, the ears not hear anything improper — than that a person should fast."

◄§ Repeating Oneself

The *Maggid* of Kelm had a number of sermons which he repeated often. An unrepentant sinner once asked him, "Rabbi, why do you keep repeating the same sermons time after time?"

"Why," retorted the *Maggid*, "do you repeat the same sins time after time?"

So What?

A man once came crying to R' Asher of Stolin. He had committed one of those sins for which repentance is insufficient to expunge the sin.

R' Asher told him, "What difference should that make to you? It is your duty to repent regardless, and not to worry about whether your repentance is accepted or not. If you're afraid that you'll lose your place in the World-to-Come, *Chazal* tell us that an hour of repentance in this world is greater than the entire World-to-Come."

The Biggest Sinner

R' Menachem Mendel of Kotzk used to say, "A person who studies with less than his full effort, or prays today just because he prayed yesterday, may be less worthy than a thief. The latter, at least, makes full effort to steal since he must eat today."

The Chain that Binds

At the time of the expulsion of the Jews from Spain, numerous Jews pretended to convert to Catholicism to save their lives. Among these was one Don Manuel, a close adviser and friend of King Ferdinand.

Eventually, the Inquisition found out that Don Manuel was in fact still a practicing Jew, and he was sentenced to death by fire.

At the time appointed for Don Manuel's punishment, King Ferdinand himself appeared to witness it. The king offered Don Manuel one last chance. "Don Manuel," said the king, "if you promise me that you will become a good Catholic and never again adopt any Jewish practices, I will spare you."

Don Manuel looked around wildly and began shouting, "The chain! The chain! How can the chain be broken?"

"What chain?" said the king. "Don Manuel, there is no chain holding you down."

"The chain!" screamed Don Manuel. "The chain that links me to my fathers Avraham, Yitzchak, and Yaakov — how can the chain be broken? How can I agree to allow that chain to be broken?"

Then, with *Shema Yisrael* on his lips, Don Manuel went to his death.

⋙ A Simple Reckoning

R' Shalom Mordechai of Barzan said: "If I am asked whether a certain item is permitted and I mistakenly rule that it is, that is only a sin between man and Hashem. On such sins I can do *teshuvah*, and Yom Kippur then grants me forgiveness. On the other hand, if I forbid something which is permitted, that is a sin between both man and Hashem and between man and his fellow man. And on sins between man and his fellow man, Yom Kippur does not bring forgiveness."

⋙ All the More

R' Simchah Zissel of Kelm used to say: "One who attempts to seduce another into idol worship is subject to the death penalty, whether or not he succeeds. Since we know that Hashem's mercy is much greater than His wrath, imagine the reward for one who tries to bring another person to *teshuvah,* even if he does not succeed!"

⋙ Pomegranates

R' Baruch of Medzhibozh could not tolerate people who acted as if they were piety personified. He used to say: "*Chazal* tell us that even the sinners of Israel are as full of *mitzvos* as a pomegranate is full of seeds. From this we can see that a person can be as full of *mitzvos* as a pomegranate is full of seeds — and still be a sinner."

≈§ Not a Torah Game

When R' Yechiel Michel of Gustinin was a young man, he begged a friend to teach him to play chess. Almost immediately, however, he stopped his lessons. "I learned," said R' Yechiel Michel, "that one of the rules of chess is that once a person has made a move he is not permitted to take it back. That is against everything we believe. For Jews, no act is absolutely final. It is never too late for a person to do *teshuvah* — to repent."

≈§ Who Has the Right to Complain?

A young man who had spent many years in Volozhin Yeshiva became a freethinker. Years later, he was staying at a certain inn when he met the *Netziv*, his former *rosh yeshiva*. "How are you? How are things going?" asked the *Netziv*.

"Very well, thank you," replied the former student. "I'm in excellent health and earning a good living. I have no complaints to Hashem."

"That isn't the question," said the *Netziv*. "The question is whether Hashem has any complaints about you."

≈§ How to Prepare for a Trip

Prior to leaving on a journey, the Vilna Gaon studied the second chapter of *Mesilas Yesharim*, which deals with the avoidance of sin, thirteen times. Only then did he leave his home.

≈§ Be Practical!

A wealthy Jew made a special trip from California to consult with the previous Lubavitcher Rebbe, R' Yosef Yitzchak Schneerson, about a major business venture. After hearing him out, the Rebbe advised him to take a certain course of action.

Afterwards, the Rebbe began talking to the man about his personal life and soon realized that there were many areas in which the man and his family were quite remiss in the performance of *mitzvos*. The Rebbe, of course, urged the man to change his ways.

"Rebbe, you don't understand," replied the man. "While your ideas are very nice, they're simply not practical in the circumstances in which I live."

"I don't understand you," said the Rebbe. "You travel three thousand miles to come to me for my business advice and are willing to accept my advice even though I'm far from a businessman. But when it comes to *mitzvos*, which is the area in which my ancestors and I have specialized, you're not willing to listen to me."

⋅§ *The Scarecrow*

When R' Naftali of Ropshitz became *rav* of the town, he told the community, "You all know that a scarecrow is nothing but some clothes on a stick designed to resemble a man and to frighten birds away. Well, I am like that scarecrow. I'm only a stick, but when I am dressed as a *rav*, it will hopefully instill in you a fear of sin."

The
Yetzer Hara

⌘ A Fool He Isn't

Among the chassidim of R' Naftali of Ropshitz was a man
known by one and all as "Leibel the Fool." Leibel went to
great lengths to appear "super-pious." One day, he approached R' Naftali, proudly displaying the hair shirt he was
wearing to make himself feel uncomfortable. R' Naftali
exclaimed upon seeing him, "He's not a fool at all."

Leibel thought R' Naftali was referring to him, but the latter
soon disabused him of that mistaken impression. "Actually,"
said R' Naftali, "I wasn't referring to you. We know that
Shlomo refers to the *yetzer hara* as 'an old and foolish king.'
If the *yetzer hara* was able to persuade someone to walk
around the whole day with a hair shirt, he's not a fool at all!"

⊷§ A Guter Yid

One of the opponents of chassidism told R' Simchah Bunim of Pshischa that the desire to become what chassidim call *a guter Yid* — a good Jew — was as much a lust as any other. "That is indeed true," replied R' Simchah Bunim, "but to attain that lust, a person must first rid himself of every other lust."

⊷§ A Sure Cure

The chassidim of R' Naftali of Ropshitz once begged him for some way to prevent the *yetzer hara* from pursuing them. "I can assure you," said R' Naftali, "that the *yetzer hara* won't pursue you if you don't pursue it."

⊷§ Having Conquered the Yetzer Hara . . .

An elderly chassid told R' Chanoch of Alexander, "Rebbe, after struggling for decades, I have finally overcome my *yetzer hara*. Now I wish to attain the level of chassidus — piety." R' Chanoch replied with a smile, "It's not that you've overcome your *yetzer hara*. If you had the strength, you would sin the same way as before. In your case, your *yetzer hara* has simply been transformed into pride."

⊷§ How Do You See the Yetzer Hara?

"The *yetzer hara*," said R' Simchah Bunim of Pshischa, "should be viewed as an executioner with his sword drawn, poised to cut off our heads at any moment."

"Rebbe," asked one of the chassidim, "what if I can't see the *yetzer hara* that way?"

"That's a sign," said the Rebbe, "that he has already cut off your head."

﹌ In the Most Unexpected Places

R' Naftali of Ropshitz was once asked, "Rebbe, where does the *yetzer hara* dwell?"

"It dwells," he said, "in exactly those places where you don't think it does."

﹌ It Depends on What You Overlook

The *Chafetz Chaim* used to say: "A pious Jew always worries that he might have inadvertently committed a sin. One who is not pious worries that he might not be aware of something which is permitted."

﹌ Little by Little

R' Yosef Yitzchak of Lubavitch used to say: "If you see someone lost in the woods, you can be sure it didn't happen suddenly. At first he left his home and walked on the road leading through the woods. Then he moved away from the road little by little, until he was hopelessly lost. And the same is true for the *yetzer hara*. At first it teaches the person to diverge just a little from proper behavior, and then more and more, until he loses his bearings entirely."

﹌ That Isn't the Way to Go About It

A young man came to R' Yisrael of Ruzhin and begged him to help him find a way to break the *yetzer hara*. "You can break your back or your leg, and even then you will not break your *yetzer hara*," replied the Rebbe. "But if you *daven*, learn, and perform the *mitzvos* with *kavanah*, the *yetzer hara* will disappear by itself."

﹌ The Clenched Fist

R' Nachman of Breslov used to say: "The *yetzer hara* is like a person who circulates among a crowd with his fist clenched tight, asking each person what he thinks is inside the clenched fist. Each person believes he is holding exactly what the person wants and craves. Finally, the *yetzer hara* opens his hand revealing that there is nothing inside."

∽§ Try, Try Again

R' Moshe of Kobrin was once asked what a person who had submitted to his *yetzer hara* should do. "When you fall off a horse," said R' Moshe, "what do you do?"

"I immediately climb on again, Rebbe," answered the man.

"You must do the same with the *yetzer hara*," said R' Moshe. "If you have tried to vanquish him and failed, you must try and try and try again."

∽§ Who Is Talking?

A woman came to see R' Aharon of Karlin. As soon as she entered the room, she burst into tears. When she had calmed down somewhat, she told the Rebbe that a few years earlier she had arranged a match for her daughter with a certain young man. As was the custom in those days, the marriage had been made conditional on the payment of a certain sum of money to the young man. For years she had been scrimping and saving to collect the amount involved, but now the young man had gotten tired of waiting and told her that unless the entire sum was arranged in a few days, the wedding would be called off.

The Rebbe asked her how much money she needed, went over to the closet in his room, took out the amount she had specified, and gave it to her. A few days later, the same woman came to the Rebbe, again in tears: How could she marry off her daughter, she sobbed, if she didn't have the money to pay for a bridal dress? Again R' Aharon went over to the closet, took out the necessary sum, and gave it to her.

When R' Aharon's wife heard about this, she expressed great surprise. "I can understand your giving the mother money the first time," she said. "To ensure that a Jewish girl marries is a great *mitzvah*. What I don't understand is why you gave the mother money for a bridal dress. The groom did not threaten to call off the ceremony because the girl didn't have a bridal dress. The money could have better been distributed among the poor."

"At first I thought that exact thing," said R' Aharon. "As I went over to the closet the second time, I considered whether I might be doing more good by giving the money to the poor, so that they could buy food for their hungry children. Then I analyzed my question further. Who was speaking? Was it my *yetzer tov* — my good inclination? If so, why had the same question not occurred to me when the mother came the first time? After all, isn't feeding hungry children at least as important as enabling a girl to be wed? Why was it that I only thought of that now? I decided that the question could have come only from my *yetzer hara* and therefore decided to ignore it."

✺§ Who Is the Pursuer?

R' Pinchas of Koretz once came into the *beis midrash* and saw a group of his chassidim talking. He approached and asked them what *sugya* in the *Gemara* they were discussing. There was a moment of embarrassed silence until one of the chassidim said, "Rebbe, we are devising plans to foil the *yetzer hara* which pursues us constantly."

R' Pinchas told them: "You are not yet at the stage where the *yetzer hara* pursues you. Meanwhile, it is you who are pursuing it."

✺§ Give It Time

R' Yitzchak of Worka approached a certain miserly man for a contribution to a worthy cause. The man refused point-blank. R' Yitzchak neither said a word nor moved from his place.

"Rebbe," said the man impatiently, "I told you I won't give you a thing!"

R' Yitzchak remained seated.

"Rebbe," said the man angrily, "I told you once and for all that I'm not going to give you anything! There's no reason for you to wait."

"There is a reason for me to wait," said R' Yitzchak. "As we know, man has two inclinations — a good one and a bad one. The bad inclination — the *yetzer hara* — comes to the person on the day he is born, while the good inclination only comes to him when he turns thirteen. Now, as the older of the two, your *yetzer hara* spoke first, as is only fitting. Now I'm waiting for your *yetzer tov* to speak."

These words moved the man, and he contributed to the cause.

✂§ Keeping the Scales Balanced

The *Chafetz Chaim* had a student who was a great Torah scholar and extremely poor. The student would constantly tell him, "If I ever become wealthy, I will always be very generous in giving *tzedakah*."

The *Chafetz Chaim* would listen and nod his head.

Eventually, the student moved to St. Petersburg, went into business and became very rich. But the richer he became, the stingier he became, and he ignored appeals for *tzedakah*.

When the *Chafetz Chaim* was in St. Petersburg, his former student came to visit him. The *Chafetz Chaim* asked, "How are you? What are you doing?"

"Thank God," the former student replied, "everything is fine."

"And do you give *tzedakah*?" asked the *Chafetz Chaim*.

The man turned red.

"Let me tell you a story," replied the *Chafetz Chaim*:

There was once a peasant who came to the big city to buy various supplies. He entered a mill and told the miller, "I want to buy flour."

"The sacks of flour are in front of you," replied the miller. "Put as much as you want in the cup and empty it into the balance pan of my scale."

The peasant, who was somewhat dim-witted, took a cup of flour and emptied it onto the balance pan. Then he emptied another and another. His pile of flour kept getting higher and higher. Meanwhile, the miller kept placing weights in the other pan. Finally, the peasant stopped.

"That will be five rubles," the miller told him.

"Five rubles?" blurted out the peasant. "All I wanted was one ruble's worth."

"Fool! said the miller. "If you only wanted a ruble's worth, why did you keep heaping more and more onto the scale? Didn't you see that every time you added flour to your pan I was adding a weight to my pan?"

"As a person keeps gaining more and more money," said the *Chafetz Chaim*, "he often forgets that the more money he has, the greater becomes his *yetzer hara* — his evil inclination.

Mashiach

⋖ A Time to Weep, Not Rejoice

When the Austrian emperor granted the Jews equal rights before the law, there was widespread rejoicing among the Jewish population. The *Chasam Sofer*, though, was very depressed by the news. His followers asked him, "Rebbe, why are you so upset when everyone else is so happy?"

"My sons," he said, "let me tell you a story. There was once a king who had a very close friend, one whom he loved dearly and whose advice he always sought. The friend allied himself with plotters against the king and was caught.

" 'You really deserve to die,' the king told him, 'but as we have been friends for so many years, I cannot kill you. Instead you will be imprisoned for a long period of time. Eventually, however, I will pardon you.'

"The man was dragged off and flung into a filthy dungeon with no light, and rats scampering about. Year after year, the friend languished in his dungeon, mourning and waiting for the king to fulfill his promise and pardon him.

"One day, the man heard a loud noise outside. Listening closely, he discerned the voices of the king's men. He was overjoyed. Surely the king had finally decided to pardon him.

"The dungeon was opened, and the king's men came in. 'His majesty has decided to make things easier for you,' one said. 'The dungeon will be thoroughly cleaned, and a window will be built so that you can have light throughout the day.'

"The man was crushed and began crying hysterically. 'Aren't you happy about the change?' one of the king's men asked him.

" 'On the contrary,' he said. 'Up till now, I thought I might be freed at any minute. Now who knows how long it will be until I'm finally freed.'

"And that is how I feel about the emperor's decrees," said the *Chasam Sofer*. "*Chazal* tell us that when our troubles seem beyond endurance, *Mashiach* will come at any moment. Now that our lot has been made easier, who knows what that means as far as *Mashiach's* coming? That's why I am weeping."

ᴴᴥ§ *Let's Keep It a Secret*

A man who lived in Pshischa suffered from delusions that the local constable was Eliyahu the Prophet and that he himself was no less than *Mashiach*. R' Simchah Bunim summoned the man.

"Who am I?" he asked.

"You're the rebbe of the town," answered the man.

"Well, if I'm the rebbe, can you imagine that both Eliyahu the Prophet and *Mashiach* are living in my town without my knowing about it?"

"I am sure, rebbe," the man replied, "that you do know it, but have your own reasons for not revealing it to anyone."

"If that's the case," said R' Simchah Bunim, "I suggest you learn from me and don't reveal to anyone that you are *Mashiach*."

The man thought it over for a time and from then on made no more mention of his delusions.

✑ Our Generation

R' Shmelke of Nikolsburg was once asked, "Rebbe, if *Mashiach* didn't come in the generations of such men as David and Shlomo, why should he come now?"

"When a king wishes to capture a city," said R' Shmelke, "he first sends in his best troops, to be sure that he has the manpower necessary to take the city. Once the city has been taken, however, and there is a need to clear all the rubble before rebuilding, even the lowliest troops can be used. Our generation," he said, "is that generation which will rebuild the city after the previous generations captured it for us."

✑ That Question Will Also Be Answered

A wealthy man once asked R' Yitzchak Blaser, one of the great *Mussar* figures, if he really believed that *Mashiach* can come tomorrow, R' Yitzchak replied that he did.

"I don't see how that's possible," the man continued. "*Chazal* tell us that *Mashiach* will only come when all money has disappeared. Of course, it is possible for some people to lose all their money. But wealthy people such as myself, who have holdings in many places, cannot possibly lose everything. If we lose money in one place, we will still have assets in many other places."

"Your problem is no problem," said R' Yitzchak. "And even if a prophet came tomorrow and told me that *Mashiach* would not come that day I wouldn't believe him. I can even prove this to you. Hashem told Avraham that his descendants would be enslaved for four hundred years, yet they left Egypt after two hundred and ten years. The promise and what actually occurred seem irreconcilable, yet our Sages explained the contradiction. By the same token, if *Mashiach* comes tomorrow, I am fully convinced that our Sages will have an explanation of how *Mashiach* came even though there was still money left."

◄§ *Waiting for Mashiach*

R' Moshe Teitelbaum waited impatiently for the arrival of *Mashiach*. Whenever there was any tumult in his town, he immediately went to see if it might be that *Mashiach* had come. He begged all of those around him to inform him immediately if anything unusual took place, for strange events might be a harbinger of *Mashiach*.

Before Pesach, he used to prepare a basket with *matzos* and wine so that he would be ready, at a moment's notice, to leave as soon as *Mashiach* arrived, and each night, he sat at the window prior to going to sleep, watching and waiting for *Mashiach*.

◄§ *Why Mashiach Hasn't Come Yet*

R' Eliezer of Rozniatov asked R' Menachem Mendel of Kosov, "Rebbe, why has *Mashiach* not come?

"The answer," said R' Menachem Mendel, "lies in the verse in *Shmuel* (I, 20:27), 'Why has the son of *Yishai* not come today or yesterday?' Why hasn't he come? Because our today is like our yesterday."

◄§ *The Uniqueness of Mashiach's Time*

A great rabbi was once asked, "Rebbe, we are told that in the time of *Mashiach* the wolf will lie down with the lamb, and all animals will live in harmony with one another. What is so special about that? After all, didn't that already occur in Noach's ark? There, all the animals were gathered together under one roof, and all lived amicably together."

"There is a marked difference between the two," answered the rabbi. "In the case of Noach's ark, they all lived together amicably because otherwise they would have died in the flood. That was a temporary truce among the animals.

"This phenomenon is not only true for the animals. We ourselves have seen that when a country is in danger or at war with another, all the different factions join together to overcome the danger to their country.

"At the time of *Mashiach*, on the other hand, even though all the animals will not be in mortal danger, they will still live in peace with one another. And by the same token, at the time of *Mashiach* all of mankind, with all its rivalries and disputes, with all its parties and factions, will join together into a single unified whole."

ᦤ *Profit and Loss*

A man once said to the *Chafetz Chaim*, "Rabbi, I can hardly wait for *Mashiach*. When he comes, there will be no *yetzer hara*, and it will be so easy to perform the *mitzvos* and study Torah."

"On the contrary," said the *Chafetz Chaim*, "*Chazal* tell us that when *Mashiach* comes, there will be no such thing as reward and punishment for one's actions. Take, for example, merchants. They know that if the price is low they will have many more customers, but will earn far less per customer. They prefer fewer customers and a larger profit margin. As long as there is a *yetzer hara*, it may be much harder to perform *mitzvos*, but the reward for doing so is great. Once *Mashiach* comes, however, the reward for performing *mitzvos* will be negligible."

◄§ The Labor Pangs of the Mashiach

R' Yisrael of Ruzhin explained the great calamities suffered by the Jews of his generation as follows: "When a woman is in her eighth month of pregnancy and suffers pain, we do everything possible to alleviate the pain to prevent her from giving birth prematurely. When the time comes, however, for a woman to give birth and she feels the pangs of labor, we don't do anything to prevent the labor. After all, her time has come. And the same is true today. We are fast approaching the time of *Mashiach*, and that is why we feel the pangs of labor so keenly and cannot alleviate them."

Between Man and his Fellow Man

Gemilas Chassadim

⋅৺ *A Different Standard*

In former times, one of the duties of each town's *shochet* was to take care of the needs of travelers passing through the town.

The chassidim of R' Yisrael of Ruzhin once complained to the Rebbe that the *shochet* of a nearby town refused to give *tzedakah* to the poor who came to his door. R' Yisrael investigated and found that it was true. He immediately ordered the man to stop working as a *shochet*.

"Rebbe," the man argued, "there are many people in the town much wealthier than I who give far less. Why do you expect so much more from me?"

"You're absolutely right," said R' Yitzchak, "but you are held to a higher standard. We find in the Torah next to the discussion of an *ir ha'nidachas* — a town so corrupt that it and all its inhabitants must be destroyed — a Divine promise: 'He will be merciful to you and make you merciful.' Why is this blessing found here? The answer is that Hashem was afraid that those involved in wiping out an entire town might lose their mercy and compassion. Thus He gave those involved a special blessing.

"Similarly, your job as a *shochet* could lead you to become cruel to humans as well as animals. To counter this, a *shochet* is required to help others. Thus, anyone who doesn't have mercy on the poor cannot serve as a *shochet*."

ᴥᶳ *A True Leader*

A large fire once broke out in Brisk, destroying many homes. Especially hard hit were the shacks belonging to the poor. The first night after the fire, R' Chaim, whose own home had emerged unscathed, slept in the *shul* with those whose homes had been destroyed.

When asked why he was sleeping in the *shul,* R' Chaim replied, "I cannot sleep in my own bed when so many are homeless. I intend to sleep in the *shul* until everyone has a roof over his head. If I remain in my own house, who knows how long it will take the community to raise the necessary funds to rebuild the homes of all the poor, the widows, and orphans. But if it is known that I too will sleep in the *shul* until the work is completed, the fundraising will go much faster."

Only when the last home had been rebuilt did R' Chaim move back into his own house.

ᴥᶳ *Advice to Fit the Situation*

A troubled woman once sought the advice of R' David Kronglas, the *mashgiach* of Ner Israel. The woman did most of the talking. Nevertheless, when she left, she looked much more at ease than when she had arrived. After the woman had left, R' David's wife asked him why she looked so much more cheerful, given that she had done most of the talking. R' David answered, "She didn't really come to ask my advice. She simply needed someone with whom to share her troubles, so I let her speak as long as she wanted to."

◆§ At Least He Keeps One Rule

In Slonim, there once lived a very wealthy man who gave no money to *tzedakah*. R' Eizel Charif, the *rav* of Slonim, once said about him, "At least he keeps one aspect of the laws of *tzedakah*. One is not required to give so much that the poor man becomes wealthy, and he is scrupulous in this regard."

◆§ Caring for Widows

Each morning, R' Moshe Leib of Sassov visited the homes of all the widows and orphans in town to wish them a good morning and find out if they needed anything.

◆§ Different Criteria

A friend once visited R' Chaim Ozer Grodzenski of Vilna on Sukkos. R' Chaim Ozer explained that he was in very poor health and thus exempt from eating in the *sukkah*, and asked his guest to please take some food and eat in the *sukkah* by himself.

As he was eating, the visitor heard someone shuffling painfully into the *sukkah*. When he looked up, he saw R' Chaim Ozer. The man protested that R' Chaim Ozer should not have troubled himself in his condition. R' Chaim Ozer replied, "It's true that I'm exempt from being in the *sukkah*, but I still have the obligation of *hachnasas orchim* — being hospitable to one's guests. It's not very hospitable to have one's guests eat alone.

"Furthermore," said R' Chaim Ozer, "I have clear proof that my pain does not excuse me from *hachnassas orchim*, for we are told that on the third day after Avraham's *bris milah*, when the pain was the most severe, he ran to fulfill the *mitzvah* of *hachnasas orchim*."

ᴥ§ Feeding the Soul

R' Chaim of Sanz once noticed that one of his chassidim was not served anything at the *tisch*. The chassid protested that the oversight was meaningless since he had not come to eat. "The soul also doesn't come into this world, Heaven forbid, in order to eat," said the Rebbe with a smile. "But if one doesn't feed it, it soon withers away."

ᴥ§ Following Orders

R' Shmuel Dov Ber of Lubavitch once asked one of his chassidim to donate a large sum of money to a worthy cause. The man found all types of excuses as to why he could not afford it: Business was bad, debtors had not paid him, the amount represented a tenth of all he owned, etc.

R' Shmuel Dov Ber listened to all the excuses and told the man, "When you ask me to pray to Hashem on your behalf, you expect Hashem to listen to you and grant you whatever you want. But when I ask you for something, rather than listening to me you come up with all types of excuses."

ᴥ§ Hachnasas Orchim

A man once visited the *Maggid* of Trisk. He appeared to be a *talmid chacham*, and the entire family treated him with the highest respect. In the end, however, he was found to be a swindler, and the *Maggid's* family was crestfallen at having been deceived.

The *Maggid,* however, received the news with equanimity. "After all," he told his family, "when Hashem wanted to help

Avraham fulfill the *mitzvah* of *hachnasas orchim*, He sent him three angels — and angels don't need to eat or drink. From this we can see that it is not the person to whom one shows hospitality that makes the difference. What counts is the intentions of the person who offers the hospitality."

◄§ Helping Oneself

R' Gedalyah Schorr was riding the subway one morning when he saw someone trying to study the *daf yomi*. The man was having difficulty, so R' Gedalyah went over to him and said, "I haven't had the opportunity to learn the *daf* today. Would you mind if I study along with you?" They spent the rest of the train ride learning the *daf* together. The man recalled later that the entire time R' Gedalyah made the man feel that he was doing R' Gedalyah a favor.

◄§ No More Than Your Duty

R' Elya Chaim, the *rav* of Lodz, had the ability to convince the wealthy Jews of Lodz to donate generously to various worthy causes. Some of the large contributors felt that their generosity gave them the right to dictate to R' Elya Chaim.

Whenever they tried, R' Elya Chaim told them, "*Rashi* comments that the *chasidah* — the stork — derives its name from the fact that it is involved in *chassidus* — good deeds — with its fellows. If so, why is it listed as one of the non-kosher species? The answer is that it is unkosher because it feels that what it does is *chassidus* — above and beyond what it is required to do — whereas in reality it is only doing its duty. And the same is true with you. When you give a large sum of money, you are doing nothing more than your duty, for you have the means to do so."

✑ Take Your Pick

R' Moshe Yitzchak, the *Maggid* of Kelm, was once invited to speak in a large town. Before ascending the *bimah,* he asked the local *rav* if there was any special problem that should be addressed. "Indeed there is," said the *rav.* "We have a hospital for the poor, but it's in danger of closing because the rich have not donated enough money to keep it going."

When R' Moshe Yitzchak got up to speak, he addressed the people as follows:

"My friends, we have a tradition that the *Shechinah* — Hashem's Divine presence — hovers over the bed of the sick. Once the *Shechinah* came to complain to Hashem, 'I simply have no more strength to go on. I constantly find myself in the homes of the poor, where the people lie sick, tossing and turning on their broken-down beds. All about are women and children who are cold, weary, and hungry. I cannot continue this way.'

" 'You are absolutely right,' agreed Hashem. 'I will transfer illness to the rich.' And so it was done. The *Shechinah* felt no need to complain any more. After all, it was now stationed in warm comfortable places, with people lying on clean sheets and in homes filled with the best of everything.

"But now the rich people began to complain. They did not want to have to suffer the pain of illness. To solve their problem, they finally hit upon a brilliant idea. They would build hospitals for the poor. These hospitals would offer clean, hygienic conditions for them. In such an environment, the *Shechinah* could not complain. No sooner said than done. They built a hospital, moved the poor into it, and sickness soon left their midst.

"Now, however," he concluded. "the hospital is in danger of closing. If it does, the poor who now have such good conditions will be forced to return to their own homes. Again the *Shechinah* will have a valid complaint about the depressing conditions in which it finds itself. And again Hashem will have to assuage its feelings by moving sickness back to the rich.

"If you don't want that to happen, you have but one choice — to pledge right now, so that there will be enough funds to keep the hospital running."

◆§ The Translator

An elderly woman was often seen coming to R' Moshe Feinstein's office bearing an envelope. Later it became known that this woman had a sister in Russia, who wrote letters to her in Russian. Despite his immense burdens, R' Moshe translated the letters she received and then wrote her replies.

◆§ The True Importance of Money

Money was completely without importance to R' Chaim of Brisk. He was once at the wedding of the children of two wealthy men. The next day the two fathers came to him and handed him a sealed envelope filled with money. As soon as they left, a worthy, poor man came in and told R' Chaim of his desperate plight. Without another word, R' Chaim handed the man the still-sealed envelope.

◆§ A Better Understanding of the Grace After Meals

Before World War II, a poor European *rav* found himself stranded in a town in the United States. Not knowing whom to approach, he decided to appeal to the rabbi of the town. He went over to the *shul*, and was told that the rabbi only received visitors during his office hours, twice a week. Not having any choice, the *rav* waited until the rabbi's next office hours and presented his problem to the rabbi. The rabbi gave him a donation and wished him well. As they were talking, the rabbi asked the *rav* to tell him a *dvar Torah*.

The *rav* agreed and began: "In the Grace After Meals, we thank Hashem for supporting us 'each day and each time and each hour.' I always wondered what the reason was for this threefold repetition. Now it's perfectly clear to me. We thank Hashem for helping us at all times, each day and every hour, and not only during office hours."

ᴥᴮ *What Type of Hospitality Do You Offer?*

R' Levi Yitzchak of Berdichev once arrived in a town very late at night. Seeing a light in one of the homes, he knocked on the door, and the owner opened it. R' Levi Yitzchak asked for a corner to spend the night, but the man turned him down even though he was obviously wealthy. "Go and ask the *melamed* two streets down," he said, and abruptly shut the door in R' Levi Yitzchak's face. R' Levi Yitzchak went to the *melamed's* home and was immediately invited in. The *melamed*, a poor man, was more than happy to share whatever he had with R' Levi Yitzchak.

The next day, news spread through the town that R' Levi Yitzchak of Berdichev was staying at the *melamed's* home. Soon all the townsfolk gathered outside the house. Among those gathered outside was the man who had refused R' Levi Yitzchak a place to sleep the previous night. Making believe that nothing had happened, the man said, "Rebbe, there is very little room here. Why don't you stay in my home? There I can offer you your own room and the best food to be had in town."

R' Levi Yitzchak replied, "When it comes to offering hospitality, there are two kinds of people — those who follow Avraham and those who follow Lot. When the angels came to Avraham, he thought they were Arabs, yet he immediately invited them in. Lot, on the other hand, was only willing to allow them in once he was sure they were angels. Your hospitality, unfortunately, is that of Lot."

❧ Love of a Fellow-Jew

R' Shlomo of Slonim was taken to a Nazi concentration camp where the sadistic Nazi guards constantly did everything possible to torment him. Once they grabbed another Jew, tied him tightly, and then brought R' Shlomo in. Handing him a heavy club, they ordered him to beat the other Jew. Otherwise, he himself would be beaten — possibly even to death.

The Rebbe took the club and pretended to beat the man, each time stopping short a fraction of an inch from actually hitting him.

Eventually, the Germans realized what was happening, and beat R' Shlomo mercilessly for a long time. The Rebbe had placed his own life in danger rather than beat another Jew.

❧ The Last Selection

In the last days of the Warsaw Ghetto, when most of the Jews had already been driven to Treblinka, only three *rabbanim* remained in all of Warsaw — R' Menachem Ziemba, R' Shimshon Shtokhammer and R' David Shapiro. It was just then that a message was smuggled into the ghetto. Catholics were willing to smuggle the three out and hide them in safe homes until the end of the war. A reply had to be sent immediately.

The youngest, R' David Shapiro, broke the silence. "There is no place where Hashem is not found" he said. "Can we then hide from Him? I wish to go on record first, as the youngest, not obliging anyone else. I believe that we should not even debate the issue. As long as there is a Jew still living in the ghetto, I will not abandon it." The others were in full agreement. All rejected the offer out of hand, and remained in the ghetto. Miraculously, R' Shapiro survived.

Consideration for Others

≈§ A Greater Priority

One Rosh Hashanah, the *Chazon Ish* ordered that the *shofar* be blown immediately after the reading of the Torah, without the customary break in the *davening*. Nor did he allow the recitation of the psalm *Lamnatze'ach* seven times, as is usually done before the *shofar* blowing. The congregation was puzzled by these breaks with tradition. Only after *Mussaf* did the *Chazon Ish* reveal his reasons. He had heard a man say to his elderly father, "Father, please eat something. You are so weak," and the father had replied, "I have never in my life eaten before *shofar* blowing." It was for the sake of that elderly Jew that the *Chazon Ish* had sped up the prayers.

ᴇ§ A Lesson from a Tailor

For years, R' Mordechai of Neshchiz sought to have a *tallis kattan* made of wool woven in *Eretz Yisrael*. Finally, after great effort, he managed to obtain the fabric. One of his chassidim begged the rebbe to let him cut the *tallis kattan* out of the wool, and the rebbe agreed. The man was overjoyed at the opportunity. With fear and trembling, he embarked on the project. He was so nervous, however, that without realizing it, he cut out the neck portion of the cloth while the fabric was still folded in two. When the fabric was unfolded, he saw to his horror that there were two holes for the neck. The damage was irreparable. The crestfallen and terrified chassid approached his rebbe to tell him what he had done.

R' Mordechai remained absolutely calm throughout the chassid's account. "Your work was perfect," he explained. "I needed two neck holes — one for the *tallis katan* and one to teach me the importance of holding my temper in check."

ᴇ§ Broken Glass

After a wedding, R' Simchah Zissel of Kelm was seen crawling about on the floor near where the *chupah* had stood. He was looking for the broken pieces of the glass which the groom had smashed, lest someone be cut by the shards.

ᴇ§ Concern for Another's Feelings

When R' Yisrael Salanter lived in Koenigsberg, he shared a room with his student, R' Yitzchak Maltzman. Each had his own key to the room. One night the student went out to an important meeting and forgot to take his key with him. R' Yisrael saw that his student had forgotten his key and was sure that his student would not wake him by ringing the bell late at night. In order to ensure that the student would not spend the night outdoors, R' Yisrael remained outside, walking about, until R' Yitzchak returned home.

ಆ Consider the Maid

R' Yisrael Salanter made *Kiddush* as soon as possible on Friday night, in order not to keep the Jewish servant girl waiting any longer than necessary. After all, she had worked the whole day and was no doubt hungry.

One Shabbos night, as R' Yisrael was preparing to make *Kiddush*, there was a knock on the door. A man rushed in and told him that one of the local merchants had been imprisoned by the authorities, and unless quick action was taken, the man's life was in danger. R' Yisrael left the table immediately and made his way to certain officials with whom he was acquainted. After much effort, he succeeded in obtaining the merchant's release, and only close to midnight did he manage to return home and make *Kiddush* for everyone.

When he was asked why he had not been concerned about the maid that particular week, he replied, "Generally, I make *Kiddush* as soon as possible, because there is no reason why I should take my time at the maid's expense. In this case, however, where a man's life was in danger, it was the responsibility of all Jews, including the maid, to do whatever they could to save him."

ಆ Empathy

A non-religious man was eager to meet the *Chazon Ish*. He arrived at the latter's home just as the *Chazon Ish* was about to take a walk and received permission to accompany him. The *Chazon Ish* walked along silently, the man at his side. Suddenly, the *Chazon Ish* slowed down for no apparent reason. The *Chazon Ish* then explained himself, "There is a man with a limp in front of us. It is not nice to pass him and remind him of his infirmity."

⤳ First Things First

A stranger once walked into the *beis midrash* of R' Yechiel Michel of Gustinin early in the morning. The *shamash* went over to the man and asked him whether he had prayed yet. R' Yechiel Michel became angry at the *shamash* and told him:

"When a Jew who has come from afar walks into the *beis midrash* early in the morning, one doesn't ask him if he has prayed yet, but whether he has eaten."

⤳ How Would You Feel?

The head of a *gemach* — free loan fund — in Bnei Brak, came to the *Chazon Ish* with a question. People who borrowed money from the *gemach* were asked to leave something of value as a pledge — a piece of jewelry, etc. Some people had not repaid their debts for a very long time, and the *gabbai* wanted to know whether the *gemach* could sell the pledges in order to repay the debt.

The *Chazon Ish* became very upset by the question. "Imagine," he said, "that a man left his wife's jewelry as a pledge, and you sold it. The next day, the man's wife walks down the street and sees another woman wearing her jewelry. Can you imagine her emotional pain? A *gemach* must not work only according to the law. It must go above and beyond the dictates of the law."

⤳ In His Shoes

An orphan who suffered from a severe limp was caught stealing in the village of Piltz. The men who caught him began beating him. R' Pinchas Elye, one of the disciples of R' Menachem Mendel of Kotzk, happened to come by. He turned to the leader of the group and asked him:

"Were you ever an orphan?"

"No."

"Did you ever have a limp?"

"No."

"Have you ever been starving?"

"No."

"Have you ever been without a home?"

"No."

"If so," said R' Pinchas Elye, "by your actions you have violated the rule of *Chazal* that 'one may not judge another unless one is in his situation.' "

⋖§ *Jewish Blood*

R' Levi Yitzchak of Berdichev found out that the local *matzah* bakers forced the women who kneaded the dough for *matzah* to work from early morning until late into the night. He thereupon summoned the entire town and cried out: "Jews, the gentiles falsely accuse us of using gentile blood when we bake our *matzos*. That isn't true. Instead, we bake our *matzos* with the blood of Jewish women who are forced to work impossibly long hours."

⋖§ *Living Where Needed*

The Sadigerer Rebbe once reprimanded a merchant who dealt very harshly with his debtors. "Rebbe," said the man, "you should have followed the ways of the Baal Shem Tov, who lived in the forests, rather than living in the city and bothering merchants like me."

"On the contrary," said the Sadigerer, "the Baal Shem Tov lived in the forests because in his days there were brigands in the forests, and he wished to protect the innocent people from them. Nowadays, when the brigands live in the cities, I need to be here, and do what I can to help those who are defenseless."

⋖§ *Now You Know*

In R' Yisrael Salanter's yeshiva, all the students received their meals from different families who had agreed to support them in this way. The *shamash* of the yeshiva collected the meals each day from the different homes. R' Yisrael wanted to ensure that the poorest students should not feel uncomfortable taking food daily, and therefore ordered even the wealthiest students not to buy their own food, but to eat the food sent them by "their" family. Furthermore, in order to protect the students' privacy, R' Yisrael ordered the *shamash* not to reveal to the families which student they were feeding.

A wealthy carpenter, who had been sending a daily meal for some time, once asked the *shamash* to tell him who "his" student was. The *shamash* refused to divulge the information, but the carpenter became more insistent every day. Finally, the *shamash* went to R' Yisrael and told him that the carpenter was pestering him to know the name of "his" student. "If that is the case," said R' Yisrael, "I will have the student tell the carpenter, and he himself will thank the carpenter for all the help he gave him."

It so happened that the student in question was very wealthy, and only ate the meals prepared by the carpenter's wife because R' Yisrael required that all students do so. Taking two of his friends, the student went to the carpenter's house. When they were admitted, the student told the carpenter, "R' Yisrael has agreed to tell you the identity of the student to whom you sent food, but he insists that you tell him exactly what the meals have cost you until now."

The carpenter stammered that he had no idea what the cost had been and that only his wife would know. The wife was called in to work out the cost of each meal. When she had finished, the student who had been receiving the meals then announced, "I am the one to whom you sent the meals. I am certainly not in need of food from others, but accept it because R' Yisrael told me to. I am deeply grateful to you for having sent food to me each day, and I am now prepared to pay for everything I ate." With that, he took out twice the amount that had been calculated and laid it on the table. The three students then departed.

The carpenter and his wife were deeply ashamed of their actions, and could think of no way to rectify what they had done. Finally, they went to see R' Yisrael and begged him to take the money back. R' Yisrael, however, told them, "What's done is done. I insisted that all students receive their meals from others, and that no person should know to whom he was sending his food. You, however, insisted on knowing who your student was. I have fulfilled your wish, and now you know. You have been paid back both the principal and interest for your trouble."

The couple broke into tears, offered to supply two meals daily, and promised never to try to find out who was receiving their meals. Realizing that they had learned their lesson, R' Yisrael allowed them the privilege of continuing to send meals to the yeshiva students.

◈ *Never Too Black*

R' Yisrael Salanter was known for his punctuality. Thus all were very surprised when he was late for his regular *shiur* one day. His students realized that something unusual must have happened, and they went to look for him. Finally, they found him on a bridge talking to a young woman. Sensing that it was not a proper time to interrupt, the students returned to the *beis midrash*.

Sometime later, R' Yisrael revealed to his students what had happened. The young woman had lost her two children in a plague, and her husband had lapsed into a deep depression as a result. Their only horse had died, and with it their entire means of earning a livelihood. The woman had been about to throw herself off the bridge into the river when R' Yisrael saw her standing there distraught. R' Yisrael stayed with her for a very long time until he was sure that she had fully calmed down. He stressed repeatedly that she was still young and could have more children.

The following year, R' Yisrael was invited to the *bris* of the young woman's son.

ᴥᴤ Not at the Chazan's Expense

One year when the second day of Rosh Hashanah fell on Friday, the *gabbaim* of R' Yisrael Salanter's *shul* came to him and asked, "Rabbi, which of the *piyutim* may be skipped so that the people can prepare for Shabbos?"

"They may all be skipped," replied R' Yisrael, "including *U'nesaneh tokef*. The only exceptions are the *piyutim* in *Malchuyos, Zichronos,* and *Shofaros*." The *gabbaim* wondered why those *piyutim* were different. "Because they are said silently," explained R' Yisrael, "and give the *chazan* time to rest."

ᴥᴤ They Must Not Know

The *Chazon Ish* and his *talmid*, R' Shlomo Cohen, once entered an apartment building. As they stood in the stairwell, they heard a loud argument between a husband and wife. The *Chazon Ish* rushed out of the building, and R' Shlomo Cohen dashed after him. When the two had gone some distance, R' Shlomo asked the *Chazon Ish* why he had run out so fast. "I was afraid that the couple might see us and realize that I knew about their quarrel. That would certainly have embarrassed them terribly."

ᴥᴤ At What Price?

R' Yisrael Salanter railed against those who awakened their servant girls to prepare a hot drink for them before going to *Selichos* early in the morning. In those days, the women who worked as maids were generally widows or orphans, who were forced to do so in order to survive. "If you waken your maid to prepare a glass of tea for you," he said, "you are transgressing the law against oppressing the widow and orphan."

~§ Unsatisfied Hunger

It had been a long and hot fast day, and R' Yechiel Meir of Gustinin's whole family was gathered to break the fast, except for R' Yechiel Meir himself. A short while later he came home, accompanied by a wandering beggar. R' Yechiel Meir's family was eager to know where he had been. He explained, "Just like you, I felt a need to still my hunger after the long fast. You no doubt hungered for food, but I hungered to do the *mitzvah* of welcoming a guest."

~§ Preparing

A few days before R' Simcha Zissel of Kelm died, he asked that all his clothes be washed. He had requested that his clothes be distributed to the poor, and he wanted to be sure that they received clean clothes.

~§ The Best Possible Day

R' Rafael of Barshad made great efforts to make peace between quarreling parties — husbands and wives, business partners, friends who had a falling-out. On *Tishah B'Av*, he came to the home of a man who had been involved in a quarrel with another man to try to patch things up.

"Rebbe," said the man, "must this be done today? Can't it wait for tomorrow?"

"On the contrary," said R' Rafael, "the *Beis Hamikdash* was destroyed on this very day because of *sinas chinam* — baseless hatred. It is therefore particularly important to work toward bringing peace between Jews today."

Proper Conduct

◆§ Ample Reason

One great rabbi stood for every visitor, regardless of the person's age. When asked why, he explained, "If he is older than I, he has performed more *mitzvos* than I have, and if he is younger, he has committed fewer sins."

◆§ Even Modesty Must Have Its Limit

R' David of Talna used to say: "Modesty is a very important trait, and each person must be exceedingly humble — yet even modesty has its limits, as I learned from my own experience.

"My father was an extremely great man, and hundreds of people came to seek his advice. As is the custom, they would leave sums of money for him to distribute to various holy causes.

"Soon after my father died, a wealthy follower of my father came to see me to receive my blessing. He also placed a large sum of money on the table.

"I asked him, 'Why are you leaving such a large sum of money?'

" 'It's the same amount I used to leave for your father,' he replied.

" 'Indeed, but I don't begin to approach my father's deeds,' I told him.

"Without another word, he picked up the money and left.

"From that I learned a lesson. Even modesty must have its limits."

⋙ Everything Can Be Used in Serving Hashem

R' Yitzchak of Worka used to say: "As is known, every trait — even those normally considered to be deplorable — can be used in the service of Hashem, and that is exactly why Hashem created them. For example, jealousy is normally a bad trait, but when a person is jealous for Hashem's honor it is a good trait — and the same can be said for traits such as pride, stubbornness, etc.

"There is one trait, however, that seems to have no good attached to it — heresy, the denial of Hashem, Heaven forbid. But, even heresy can be used in the service of Hashem, and, in fact, is sometimes essential. For example, if someone asks me for *tzedakah*, I am not entitled to trust in Hashem to supply the man with his needs. I am required to be 'heretical' enough to give him *tzedakah*. Hashem created this trait so that no person should feel so great a sense of faith in Him as to feel no obligation to help those in distress. In this regard, every person has to have a touch of 'heresy.' "

◆§ Everything Is Relative

R' Chaim of Kosov led his chassidim every Friday night in a spirited dance. One time, however, he injured his leg, and was unable to take part in the dancing for several weeks. When he was finally able to dance again, he told his chassidim: "I didn't stop dancing because my leg hurt. Rather, because I stopped dancing my leg hurt."

◆§ Foolish Pride

The *Tzemach Tzedek*, the third Lubavitcher Rebbe, once went to visit Jewish communities throughout the area. He was welcomed everywhere, even in *misnagdic* strongholds, and all the *talmidei chachamim* in every town and village rushed to greet him and discuss Torah with him. All were amazed at the great breadth and depth of his Torah learning.

One of his sons, who accompanied him on the trip, wrote home to his mother and confided how much he enjoyed the honor shown his father.

When the *Tzemach Tzedek* returned home after his trip, he came across his son's letter. He summoned his son and berated him for the letter.

The boy's mother came to his defense, and asked her husband, "Why are you so upset? What did he write that was so wrong?"

"You don't understand," said the *Tzemach Tzedek*. "When people honor me, it eats away at me and I feel positively sick. Yet our son writes that he enjoys the honor shown me."

◆§ How to Explain the Verses

As is known, R' Menachem Mendel of Kotzk remained secluded in his room for many years. Once he opened the door to the room, summoned his *shamash*, and asked him, "Feivel, how do people explain the statement in the

Mechilta that the Torah was only given to those who ate the *manna*?"

"Rebbe," said the *shamash*, "it's explained as meaning that the Torah was given to the people in the desert because they had no worries about how to support themselves — all their needs were met by Hashem."

"No, that's not what the *Mechilta* means at all," said the Rebbe. "In fact, it means the exact opposite. It refers to those Jews who barely eke out a living, who don't know from where their next meal will come and yet do not worry about what they'll eat tomorrow. That was exactly the case with the *manna* — the amount which fell every day was only enough for that day (except, of course, on Friday). Yet they were never worried about what they would eat tomorrow. It is for such Jews the Torah was given."

With that, R' Menachem Mendel returned to his room and locked the door.

⋅§ *It's as Easy as Aleph-Beis*

Two merchants about to enter into a business partnership came to R' Meir of Premishlan for an amulet to ensure that the partnership succeed. R' Meir took out a piece of paper. On one side he wrote the letters *aleph* and *beis*, and on the other he wrote the letters *gimmel* and *daled*. He then handed it to the merchants and told them, "This is a guaranteed formula for a successful partnership."

The merchants took the paper, read both sides, and finally turned to R' Meir. "Rebbe," they said, "we don't understand what this means."

R' Meir then explained it to them. "If you conduct the partnership with the *aleph* of *emunah* — mutual faith in one another — you will see the *beis* of *berachah* (blessing). On the other hand, if, Heaven forbid, either of you indulges in the *gimmel* of *gezeilah* — theft — it can only lead to the *daled* of *dalus* — poverty."

⋑ Keeping One's Distance

R' Yitzchak Isaac Herzog, the second Chief Rabbi of Israel, used to say: "*Chazal* say, 'Warm yourself opposite the light of the *chachamim*, but take heed of their flame lest you be burned.' Now, *Chazal* did not say that one should warm himself *in the light* but *opposite the light*.

"Take the following example: If a fire is burning, a person who stands opposite it is warmed by the fire. If he approaches too close to it — and all the more so if he touches it — he is burned by that same fire.

"This teaches us that in dealing with Torah Sages one must keep one's distance. One must always hold them in the highest respect and honor. If one draws too close to them — i.e., is too familiar with them — and even more so, if he harms them, he himself will be burned. One must always keep in mind that respect for our Torah Sages is really respect for Hashem."

⋑ My Servant and Only Mine

R' Meir Simchah of Dvinsk writes in *Meshech Chachmah* that there are only three people in the Torah who are referred to by Hashem as "My servant" — Avraham, Moshe, and Kalev ben Yefuneh. The reason is that none of the three ever addressed any human being as "my master." Yehoshua is not included in this list because he referred to Moshe as "my master, Moshe."

⋑ Only for a Limited Time

The *Yehudi HaKadosh* of Pshischa would say, "Though the *halachah* permits us to hate a sinner, that is only when he is actually committing the sin. Immediately afterwards, one must again love him."

✑ Payment Where It's Due

R' Zushia of Hanipol was extremely poor, and his entire family suffered terribly as a result. Once, his wife came to him and told him that she had been wearing the same dress for years and that it was in tatters. R' Zushia began saving and scrimping wherever possible, until he finally had saved enough money to buy fabric for a new dress and to pay a tailor to sew it.

That Friday, R' Zushia saw his wife very distressed. "What is bothering you?" he asked. "Don't you have the fabric at the tailor right now?"

His wife told him that the tailor had already brought the finished dress to her, but as he handed it to her, a sigh had escaped from his lips. "What is the problem?" she had asked. "My daughter became engaged a short time ago," the tailor began. "As I was sewing the dress, her fiance walked in and assumed that I must be sewing the dress for his bride. When he found out that the dress was for someone else, he became very angry. Now I'm afraid that the whole wedding might be called off."

"When I heard that," said R' Zushia's wife, "I immediately gave him the dress for his daughter, and now I'm again without a dress."

"And did you pay the tailor for his work?" asked R' Zushia.

"Pay him for his work? Why? I gave the dress to his daughter. Isn't that enough of a present?"

"That's no excuse," said R' Zushia. "The poor man worked the whole week for the few pennies you would pay him, and waited patiently for the dress to be finished so he could receive that money and buy food for his children. What is he supposed to do for food for Shabbos? Is he to blame that you gave his daughter a gift? You must go to him immediately and pay him his wage."

⋍ᔥ Strong or Weak?

A Jew came to R' Yechezkel of Kuzmir to ask his advice as to where he should live — in a town or a village. "The answer," said R' Yechezkel, "can be found in *Rashi*. When Moshe sent the spies to *Eretz Yisrael,* he instructed them to check if the people lived in open cities or in cities which were fortified. On this, *Rashi* comments: 'If they live in open cities, it is a sign that they are strong and rely on their own strength to defend themselves, whereas if they live in fortified cities it is a sign that they are weak.' From this we see that a person who feels himself strong — and the truly strong person is the one who is able to contain his passions — can live anywhere. If, however, he has a weak nature and can be easily swayed, he must choose a place which is fortified — where there are many other observant Jews and rabbis to lead him."

⋍ᔥ Such a Knife Cannot Be Used

The Jews of a certain village came to R' Michel of Biala and asked him to help them replace the *shochet* in their town. They explained to him that the man was totally unfit to fulfill his duties and was very lax in his observance of *mitzvos*. As R' Michel continued discussing the matter with the villagers, he came to the conclusion that all the talk about the *shochet's* piety was just an excuse. In actuality, the towns-people had quarreled with the *shochet* and wanted to get rid of him.

"You know," said R' Michel, "when one slaughters an animal, the knife used by the *shochet* has to be perfect and without a single blemish. If there is the slightest nick or imperfection in the knife, it cannot be used. And if it is used, the animal is *treif*. This is all the more true when one wishes to 'slaughter' a *shochet* who has a wife and children to support. Unfortunately, I have found that the 'knife' with which you wish to 'slaughter' the *shochet* is full of blemishes, and such a knife cannot be used for the slaughter."

❧ Such Anger Cannot Be Used

In a certain village, the rabbi and the *shochet* couldn't get along. Finally, the rabbi came to R' Shlomo Kluger and asked him to have the *shochet* removed from his position on the grounds that he was quick tempered, and *Chazal* liken an angry person to an idolater.

R' Shlomo Kluger replied, "There is no doubt that if a person becomes angry frequently he is to be condemned for it, but a far more grievous sin is seeking to deprive another of his livelihood out of anger."

❧ Testing for a Good Jew

The *Yehudi Hakadosh* used to say: "Everything can be tested to see if it is good or bad. And what is the test to determine whether one is a good Jew? It is his love for his fellow Jew. If a Jew feels that his love for his fellow Jew is increasing from day to day, he can be sure that his love and fear of Hashem is also increasing."

❧ The Beard Isn't What Makes the Difference

The *Chafetz Chaim* heard about a Jew who had shaved his beard because he felt it was a liability to him as a traveling salesman. The *Chafetz Chaim* invited the man to visit him.

"Let me tell you a story," the *Chafetz Chaim* began. "A train engine was pulling a large load of ore from the mines. On one steep incline, the train stalled. The engineer tried everything. He reversed and then moved forward time and again, but the engine simply didn't have the power to pull the heavy load up the mountain.

"A simple peasant, who had never seen a train before, stood nearby watching and volunteered to help by pushing from behind. The engineer politely explained to him that his efforts would be wasted.

"What you did by shaving your beard is similar to what the peasant tried to do," concluded the *Chafetz Chaim*. "It is already decreed in Heaven at the beginning of the year what you will earn. Any extra effort on your part will not change that. Why, then, give up your appearance as an upright Jew?"

◄§ The Greatest Mussar Work

"The greatest *mussar* (ethical) work," said R' Menachem Mendel of Kotzk, "is the *Rambam's Mishneh Torah*, which contains all the laws of how one must act. A person who lives according to the *Mishneh Torah* is involved every minute in *mitzvos* and doesn't have a moment free to sin."

◄§ The Nature of a Quarrel

"Many quarrels begin with legitimate disagreements," said R' Meir Simchah of Dvinsk, "but if allowed to continue they eventually take on a life of their own, so that those involved cannot even remember what the original argument was about. We can see this from the argument between the shepherds of Avraham and Lot. At first, the quarrel was based on the fact that there was not enough grazing land for all their herds. In time, however, the Torah tells us, they 'were unable to live together,' without any legitimate reason for their quarrel."

◄§ The Only Mitzvah That May Not Have Kavanah

"Whenever a person performs a *mitzvah*," said R' Menachem Mendel of Kotzk, "the greater his *kavanah* (intention), the greater the value of the *mitzvah*. There is only one exception to that rule, and that is the *mitzvah* of *anavah* — humility. With respect to *anavah*, one is not permitted to have any *kavanah* at all, and even the slightest degree of *kavanah* ruins the performance of the *mitzvah*."

✺ The Purpose of a Mussar Lecture

Several students of the Slabodka Yeshiva went to hear R' Itzele Peterburger deliver a *mussar* lecture. When the Alter of Slobodka heard that some of them had been moved to tears by R' Itzele's words, he reprimanded them: "Listening to R' Itzele should move you to think, not cry."

✺ The Superior Way

The *Chozeh* of Lublin was told about a certain Jew who fasted throughout the week, eating solid food only on Shabbos. The *Chozeh* responded, "There are two ways to serve Hashem: one is by constant fasting and the other by elevating one's very eating into worship. The second is undoubtedly superior."

✺ Try Again

R' Yitzchak of Worka used to say, "There are some things to which one may never resign himself. If you have tried time and again to make peace between two sides, you may not give up trying. You must try over and over. That is why Moshe repeatedly sent for Dasan and Aviram."

✺ Two Eyes

One Simchas Torah, R' Yosef Yitzchak of Lubavitch commented, "When I was four years old, I asked my father why Hashem created people with two eyes and not with one eye which could see just as well.'

"He answered, 'You've learned the *aleph-beis*. Tell me what the difference is between the letters *shin* and *sin*.'

" 'The *shin* has a dot on the right and the *sin* has a dot on the left,' I answered.

" 'The same is true with humans,' said my father. 'Certain things must be seen with the right eye and others with the left eye.'

"At that time," concluded R' Yosef Yitzchak, "I realized that the *mitzvos* of Jews must be seen with the right eye, while their sins must be seen — if at all — only with the left eye."

◈ Two Weddings

A man came to R' Zanvil Klepfish and complained, "Rebbe, my daughter is getting married. I'm going to have to invite many people, and I'm afraid that the cost of the wedding will put me into debt for many years to come."

"If you look in *Tanach*," said R' Zanvil, "you'll find mention of two wedding feasts. The first was when Lavan tricked Yaakov into marrying Leah instead of Rachel. Lavan gathered all the people of his town and made a feast. And remember that Lavan was not a very scrupulous man. The other wedding feast mentioned is that of Boaz and Ruth. Though Boaz was a very wealthy man, he gathered together only a *minyan* — ten of the elders of the town — and elders don't even eat that much.

"There's absolutely no reason for you," said R' Zanvil, "to emulate the ways of Lavan. By all means make a simpler wedding and don't plunge into debt."

◈ What One Can Learn From Poker

The Rebbe of Gustinin observed people playing poker and declared that he had learned two important principles from the game: If one has bad material, he must get rid of it as soon as possible; and if one has something good, he should keep it to himself and not show it to others.

◈ Understanding Reality

R' Meir Shapiro said: "The verse (*Devarim* 17:8) speaks of distinctions between 'blood and blood,' between 'judgment and judgment,' and between 'plague and plague.' These three distinctions hint at three questions.

" 'Between blood and blood' — Why are Jews, of all people, subject to the blood libel, even though Jews are forbidden to consume blood and must soak their meat to remove even a trace of it?

" 'Between judgment and judgment' — Why do we find generations of Jews wiped out in a single day, even though we ourselves are commanded not to kill even a cow and its calf on the same day?

" 'Between plague and plague' — Why, despite Hashem's promise that He will first send a plague to our clothes and houses as a warning, are the Jews constantly persecuted, pursued and killed?

"The answer to these questions is found in the continuation of that same verse: because 'there are quarrels among you.' "

⋙ What I Brought From Home

The disciples of the *Maggid* of Mezritch always immersed themselves in a *mikveh* before visiting their Rebbe. There was one, however, who insisted on visiting the *Maggid* prior to immersing himself in a *mikveh*. He explained, "I want the *Maggid* to see the *tumah* (impurity) with which I come, so that he can help me purify myself."

⋙ Where the True Blessing Is

A man complained to R' Baruch of Kosov that whatever business schemes he dreamed up invariably failed, and he was unable to support his family.

"My son," said R' Baruch, "you misunderstand. Nowhere in the Torah does Hashem promise success for the schemes that a person dreams up. The Torah does, however, promise that Hashem will send blessing 'upon all the work of your hands.' It is your task in life to work, not to scheme. If you work diligently, you will see a blessing from the work of your hands."

✑ How Much Pride May One Have?

The Vilna Gaon was extremely humble, in spite of his stature as the greatest Torah authority for centuries. His students once asked him about this, citing *Chazal*'s comment that a *talmid chacham* should have an eighth of an eighth of conceit.

The Gaon replied, "On the contrary, that *Gemara* shows the exact opposite. It states that one should have one of *shemoneh* (the masculine form of the Hebrew word for "eight") of a *sheminis* (the feminine form of the same word) of conceit. This is an allusion to something entirely different. It refers to *shemoneh* — the eighth *pasuk* — in the *sheminis* — the eighth *sidrah* of the Torah, which is *Vayishlach*. [*Pasuk* is masculine; *sidrah* is feminine.] That verse records Yaakov's statement, 'I am not worthy of all the mercy You have shown Your servant.' A *talmid chacham* must always remember this verse and not allow himself to become conceited."

✑ Tears and Stains

R' Yisrael Salanter was once learning Torah when a man came in to ask him a halachic question. R' Yisrael answered promptly and the man left. Immediately afterwards, those present saw that R' Yisrael was very troubled. One of those close to him finally asked what was bothering him.

"As I was speaking to the man," replied R' Yisrael, "I realized that there was a tear in my jacket sleeve and that upset me. Then I thought to myself, 'If that is how I feel when I meet a fellow human being when there is a tear in my sleeve, how much more humiliated will I feel when I meet my Maker with all the tears and stains in my soul?' "

✑ What Causes What?

A man complained to R' Avraham of Porisov that he didn't know what joy was because of his great sufferings.

"How do you know that your suffering is what causes you not to be joyful?" asked R' Avraham. "Couldn't it be because you're sad that you suffer? I suggest that you become joyful, and then your suffering will vanish by itself."

～§ What Do You Have in This World?

R' Menachem Mendel of Kotzk once asked a very miserly man, who hoarded all his wealth and spent almost nothing on himself, "What do you have in this world?"

"In this world, Rebbe," said the man, "I have very little indeed. I have but a little money, some property. . ."

"No," said R' Menachem Mendl, "whatever you have described is what you have for the World-to-Come, for you are obviously intent on not using it in this world. My question therefore remains, 'What do you have in this world?'"

～§ A Reason Not to Smoke

R' Moshe Feinstein was once asked if he had ever smoked. "No," he replied, "From the earliest age of which I have any memory, I never put anything into my mouth just for pleasure."

～§ Acting Like Hashem

Late on a bitter cold night, a knock was heard at the door of R' Moshe Leib of Sassov. Looking out the window, R' Moshe Leib saw a man dressed in rags, who could barely stand upright. His hair was unkempt, and there was a wild look in his eyes. R' Moshe Leib, however, threw open the door and welcomed in the half-frozen man. "If Hashem has room for such a man in His world," he reasoned, "surely I can find room for him in my own home."

⊷ For Whom the Clock Tolls

A man once asked R' Mordechai of Lachovich how to acquire humility. "There are many ways," replied R' Mordechai. At that moment, the clock on the wall chimed the hour. "For example," he continued, "you can learn from the clock. Each time the clock chimes, ask yourself, 'I am now an hour older. Have I improved in any way? Am I a better person?' "

⊷ Full Value

A great *tzaddik* came to buy something in a store. The storeowner immediately slashed all his prices in deference to his distinguished buyer. Sensing this, the *tzaddik* told him, "I want you to charge me the same price you charge everyone else. I came here to pay with cash, not with *yiras shamayim*."

⊷ I Wish I Could Do More

When the *shul* was built in Belz, the Belzer Rebbi, R' Shalom, participated in the actual building. He used to say, "If I had the strength, I would build the entire *shul* myself, but I am simply too weak and can only do that of which I am capable." He then went on to quote Rabbeinu Bechaye: "Whoever builds a single wall of a *shul*, or even a small part — even if he knocked in only one nail — thereby earns great merit."

⊷ A Call at Midnight

A rabbi calling from out of town needed an immediate ruling from R' Moshe Feinstein. Though it was already past midnight in New York, R' Moshe immediately picked up the phone. Before speaking, R' Moshe, who had been asleep, recited *birchas haTorah* — the blessings of the Torah. At the end of the conversation, R' Moshe apologized for having recited the *birchas haTorah* at the rabbi's expense and offered to pay for that portion of the call. He explained that he had picked up the phone prior to reciting the *berachos* for fear that the caller would hang up in the interim.

ᴥᶳ A Major Argument

The *Chafetz Chaim* and Reb Chaim Ozer Grodzenski once had a protracted argument as to who would sign first on a public proclamation. The *Chafetz Chaim* refused on the grounds that Reb Chaim Ozer was the *gadol hador.* Reb Chaim Ozer returned the compliment to the *Chafetz Chaim* and added another reason the *Chafetz Chaim* should sign first — his advanced age.

The *Chafetz Chaim* countered that R' Chaim Ozer was the head of Vilna Jewry. But R' Chaim Ozer finally prevailed on the grounds that since the *Chafetz Chaim* was a *Kohen*, he was obligated to let him sign first.

With that, the *Chafetz Chaim* finally consented to sign the proclamation first, but only on the condition that R' Chaim Ozer sign his name on the same line and not below.

ᴥᶳ Enough Already!

R' Chaim Ozer Grodzenski's wife once berated him for his excessive humility. "Even humility must have a limit," she said. "I wish I knew that limit," said R' Chaim Ozer, "for then I could fully develop this important trait."

ᴥᶳ Proper Awe

R' Meir Simchah of Dvinsk once visited Kovno. Upon hearing that the *Or Sameiach* was in town, R' Boruch Ber Leibowitz of Slabodka dressed in his Shabbos clothes to greet him. But when he came to the house where R' Meir Simchah was staying, he was so overcome with awe for one whom R'

Boruch Ber's teacher, R' Chaim Brisker, had called "prince of the Torah," that he could not enter.

◆§ Tears Wash Away Sin

R' Elimelech of Lizhensk and R' Zushia of Hanipol were brothers. These famous Rebbes had a third brother who ran an inn and tavern for the local peasants. R' Elimelech's chassidim reasoned that the third brother must also be a very holy man, and decided to see for themselves.

Arriving at the inn, they booked lodgings. To their disappointment, the innkeeper spent the whole day doing what all innkeepers do — tending to the guests' needs, serving liquor, and so on. The only thing different was that every so often he would stop what he was doing, take out a little notebook, and enter a few words. The chassidim waited in vain for some sign of exceptional piety, but there was absolutely nothing special about the man's conduct. Finally, they went to bed.

That night, as they lay in bed, the chassidim heard bitter crying coming from another room. They went into the hall to investigate and determined that the weeping was coming from the room of the innkeeper himself. From the hall, the sound of the man weeping and striking his chest was more easily discerned. Finally, one of the chassidim knocked on the innkeeper's door.

After admitting his guests, the innkeeper explained his nocturnal crying: "As I go through the day, whenever I feel I did something wrong or had an improper thought, I write it down. Each night I take out my list and seek atonement for the day's sins with much weeping. I pray that by the time my writing has been erased by my tears, my sins will be erased in Heaven."

◆§ Moshe Rabbeinu's Humility

R' Levi Yitzchak of Berdichev was asked why Moshe, who was so humble that he initially refused to lead the Jews out of

Egypt, did not balk when it came to leading them at Mount Sinai.

"Moshe saw at Sinai," R' Levi said, "that Hashem had chosen the lowest and most insignificant mountain upon which to give the Torah. He therefore realized that Hashem chooses the humble, and there was certainly no one more humble than he."

◆§ Keep Away From Lies

R' Zvi Hirsh of Zidichov used to say, "The Torah commanded us to 'keep away from lies,' but never commanded us to 'draw close to the truth.' The reason is that the closer a person becomes to being a man of truth, the more he will realize that he doesn't know the truth. The Torah instead commanded us to 'keep away from lies,' because the further we keep from them, the closer we come to the truth."

◆§ Order of Priorities

R' Levi Yitzchak of Berdichev once went collecting money for the dowry of the daughter of an impoverished *talmid chacham*. Arriving in a certain town, he went to the local *rav* for a donation. After the *rav* had heard him out, he wished him much success in his collections in the town. But of his own contribution, the *rav* did not say a word.

R' Levi Yitzchak told him, "You should learn from Avimelech. The Torah relates that 'Avimelech brought out bread and water,' and only afterward 'blessed him.' One must first give, and only then offer a blessing."

◆§ The Importance of Not Being Misunderstood

R' Akiva Eiger began one of his *teshuvos*: "I am unworthy of having a query sent from so far away. Thank God there are enough great Torah scholars in your country, the least of whom is greater than I. Furthermore, I am exceptionally busy so that I do not have time for matters not pertaining to my city. However, when I was in Romberg at a *simchah*, a friend asked me to reply to your query and I remained silent. I am afraid that I might have nodded my head slightly, which might have been construed as a promise to reply, and I am therefore making an exception to my normal practice and responding."

✺§ True Humility

Despite being universally recognized as the leading *posek* of the generation, R' Moshe Feinstein remained truly humble. Someone once criticized him for being driven to *shul* on *Erev Shabbos* after the time for candlelighting. R' Moshe praised the man, in his response, for having had the courage to express criticism, and even undertook to try to avoid riding again after candlelighting, "even though there is not the slightest hint of impropriety in doing so . . . ."

✺§ Things That Money Can't Buy

The Gerrer Rebbi laid down stringent rules for his chassidim, designed to prevent the poorer among them from having to spend inordinate amounts of money. For example, he made a rule that young married couples are not permitted to buy an apartment with more than two bedrooms in Jerusalem, where the price of housing is high. Only if they are willing to buy in another, cheaper area may they buy a larger apartment. Another rule specified the maximum number of guests families may invite to a wedding.

The story is told of a wealthy chassid who said to the Rebbe, "Rebbe, you know that I'm a wealthy man. I have many friends, and would like you to waive the rule limiting the number of guests to a wedding."

"If you're that wealthy," replied the Rebbe, "maybe you can buy yourself another Rebbe."

◄§ Why Ask Me?

The first time R' Nachum of Chernobyl visited the *Maggid* of Mezritch, he asked him, "Rebbe, what can I do to prevent myself from feeling pride?"

The *Maggid* replied, in utter sincerity, "I unfortunately have no advice to give you in this regard. A person can only give advice on a subject about which he himself knows something, but I have absolutely no knowledge of pride. I simply cannot understand how any person can be proud."

◄§ Another Way of Looking at It

R' Yitzchak of Worka once stayed at an inn where the innkeeper was extremely solicitous of his every need. "This innkeeper," said R' Yitzchak, "observes the *mitzvah* of *hachnasas orchim* — taking care of guests — properly."

"But rebbe," one of his chassidim protested, "why should you praise his *hachnasas orchim*? After all, whatever he does, he does for pay."

"That isn't so," said R' Yitzchak. "In reality, he treats everyone so well because he wishes to fulfill the *mitzvah* of *hachnasas orchim*. The only reason he takes money is so that he will be able to invite other guests to his inn in the future."

◄§ Caring Only About Oneself

"Unfortunately," said the Baal Shem Tov, "some people behave like clocks. Imagine a house in flames. All around the fire is raging, but the clock keeps ticking away, oblivious to all else that is happening. The fire comes ever closer and closer, but the clock keeps ticking. Only when the fire engulfs it, does the clock finally stop."

ᴥ Mathematicians

R' Menachem Mendel of Kotzk used to say: "*Chazal* tells us that a *talmid chacham* should have an eighth of an eighth of conceit. The problem is that some *talmidei chachamim* are very poor in mathematics."

ᴥ Do Your Own Job

R' Levi Yitzchak of Berdichev saw a man rushing about in a tremendous hurry. "What do you do, sir?" he asked the man.

"Rebbe," the man replied, "I would like to stand and talk with you but I'm very busy and simply can't spare the time."

R' Levi Yitzchak pressed him, "Could you nevertheless tell me what you do?"

The man answered impatiently, "Please don't detain me, because I'm very busy and have lots of things to do."

R' Levi Yitzchak did not let up. "I know that you are involved in many different business deals, but I am only interested in the *one* thing you do."

The man was puzzled by this strange remark until R' Levi Yitzchak explained himself. "All of your work is for one purpose — to earn enough money to support yourself. But it is Hashem who supports everyone. That is His task. Your only task in life is to serve Him. Why then are you rushing about doing His job instead of yours?"

ᴥ Starting Small

R' Menachem Mendel of Kotzk strongly believed in the need for one to constantly examine his deeds. One of his chassidim once told him that he simply had no time for introspection — his whole life he was constantly busy. "Let me give you a simple piece of advice," said R' Menachem Mendel. "Every time you go down to your cellar to get a bottle of wine, sit down there for a minute or two. Slowly, you will get into the habit of examining your deeds."

⤢ I Can Be Burned

A woman came to R' Yisrael of Vizhnitz and asked for his blessing. R' Yisrael unhesitatingly blessed the woman, wishing her all the best spiritually and materially. "Rebbe," the woman insisted, "I want another blessing — a real blessing — with you placing your hands on my head as you bless me."

"Let me ask you," questioned R' Yisrael, "When you recite the blessing on the Shabbos candles, do you place your hands on the flames?"

"Of course not, Rebbe," the woman replied. "I place my hands above the flame."

"And why don't you place them on the flame?"

"Because I'll get burned if I do so," replied the woman.

"Well, I'm afraid that if I lay my hands on your head," said R' Yisrael, "they might also get burned."

⤢ It Depends on Where It Leads

R' Meir of Premishlan once told his chassidim, "Before you follow in the path of others, first be sure you know where they are headed. For example, I was once at an inn. Outside it was snowing fiercely, and all signs of roads had been obliterated. Eventually, one of the wagon drivers, who had obviously had too much to drink, left the inn, hitched up his horses to his wagon, and went on his way. Soon another driver followed. Not seeing the road anywhere, he simply followed in the ruts made by the first driver's wagon. One by one, the other drivers did the same. Eventually, after some time, all the wagon drivers found themselves stuck in the same field, one with boulders all over, where they could barely maneuver their wagons."

Tzedakah

✒ Who's the Boss?

R' Meir of Premishlan used to warn his wealthy chassidim, "Be sure that your money is under your control, and that you are not under the control of your money."

✒ Draining the Excess

The *Binah Le'itim* states, "If a person has too much money, he is like a person with too much blood in his body. Too much blood is harmful, and can cause infection. Too much money also causes infections such as cheating and theft. When a person suffers from too much blood, there is a need to drain off the excess. By the same token, if a person has too much money, it should be drained from him and given to *tzedakah*. That is the only cure."

⋙ A Lender and a Borrower

One of the great *mussar* giants was once asked if it is permitted to borrow money even if only a miracle would allow him to repay the loan. He answered that it is only permitted if the borrower himself would also lend the same amount of money to someone in the same circumstances.

⋙ A Vicious Cycle

R' Eliyahu Chaim Meisel used to give a very large percentage of his income to *tzedakah*. His friends rebuked him, for *Chazal* tell us clearly that a person should not give away more than a fifth of his income.

"You're absolutely right," replied R' Eliyahu Chaim. "I'm in a terrible predicament and I can't find a way out. I once violated the commandment against giving more than a fifth of one's income to *tzedakah*. To atone I gave *tzedakah,* as is recommended for atonement from sin. But then I was again guilty of giving more than a fifth of my income, and again I had to give *tzedakah* as an atonement. I'm caught in a vicious cycle and don't know how to get out of it!"

⋙ Hashem Will Provide

R' Elimelech of Lizhensk was extremely humble. He once became despondent while reflecting on his deeds, with the thought that he had no merits that would entitle him to enter the World-to-Come. While thus immersed in his thoughts, his five disciples — all of whom would later head major chassidic dynasties — entered the room. It occurred to him that on the merit of five such disciples, who would surely merit the World-to-Come, he, their Rebbe, would too. For a few moments he was comforted with this thought, but then he started thinking again, "So what if I enter the World-to-Come? Since I have no merits, what will I receive there?"

At last, however, he found consolation: "It is true that I have no merits, that I am the poorest of the poor in terms of good deeds. Hashem, however, is the greatest dispenser of *tzedakah* in the world. No doubt He will give me *tzedakah*, in spite of my lack of merit."

⋖§ *I Can't Afford to Be More Particular*

Once, a man with a very shady reputation came to R' Moshe Leib of Sassov and asked him for *tzedakah*. R' Moshe Leib took out his very last coin and gave it to him. When his students questioned his actions, he explained, "Hashem gave the coin to me. Should I be more particular than He as to whom I give it?"

⋖§ *I Didn't Give Birth*

R' Meir Shapiro once asked a wealthy man for a donation for his yeshiva. The man kept him waiting outside for a long time, and in the end didn't donate any money.

As R' Meir turned to leave, he said to the man, "I didn't just give birth."

"What do you mean by that?" the man asked.

"You see," said R' Meir, "sometimes I ask someone for a donation. Though he treats me shabbily, in the end he donates a large amount. So I pray to Hashem, 'Let the lack of respect he showed be an atonement for my sins. At least he gave a sizable donation.' At other times, I am given the respect due a *talmid chacham*, but the donation is small. Again I say to myself, 'Let the small amount he gave be an atonement. At least the man shows respect for *talmidei chachamim*.' In your case, however, there is a double atonement — you neither showed respect nor gave me a donation. In the Torah, the only one we find who has to bring two offerings for atonement is a woman who has just given birth. I therefore wanted to inform you that I have not just given birth."

✒ My Thieves

R' Leib, the Alter of Shpola, would give *tzedakah* to anyone who asked. Among these were some people known by all to be thieves.

"Rebbe," he was asked, "why are you willing to give *tzedakah* even to thieves?"

"It's really quite simple," he replied. "Sometimes, in the Heavens, the 'Gates of Mercy' are locked. At times like that, I need to call on my thieves to break the locks."

✒ Don't Overdo the Salt

R' Simhah Bunim of Pshischa used to say: "Salt in moderation improves the flavor of food. If, however, one adds too much salt, the food becomes inedible. The same is true with money. In moderation, it improves one's life. If, however, a person is too wealthy, he becomes totally immersed in trying to acquire more and more money, and the entire taste of life is ruined."

✒ Drunk as Lot

A drunkard came to R' Abush of Frankfurt. "Rabbi," he said, "I have a daughter to marry off and no money. If you give me a letter of endorsement, I will be able to raise the money by collecting door to door."

R' Abush complied and wrote a strong letter of endorsement.

On the strength of the letter, the man received one very large contribution. With the money, he went to a pub where he became so drunk that he passed out. When he regained consciousness, the letter had disappeared. Crying bitterly, the man rushed to R' Abush, begging for another letter of endorsement. R' Abush had by then heard of the use to which the previous letter had been put and refused to write another one.

"Let me explain to you why," R' Abush told the man. "We know that a Jewish drunkard is referred to as being 'drunk as Lot.' Now, if we look in the Torah, we see that the first person to become drunk was Noach. Why, then, do we always link drunkenness to Lot? The answer is that Noach had no daughters to wed, so he could afford to become drunk. Lot, who had two daughters, could not afford to drink away the money he would need to arrange marriages for his daughters."

◆§ Know What You Are Missing

R' Moshe Saba, the author of *Tzror Hamor*, once asked, "Why do people rush back and forth frantically trying to earn more money, while few people rush about in an effort to gain more wisdom?" He answered, "Everyone feels that he is lacking enough money, but few people realize that they are lacking in wisdom."

◆§ Pikuach Nefesh Takes Precedence Over Shabbos

R' Hershele Lisker used to distribute the money his chassidim gave him to the poor. Sometimes, a non-observant Jew sought R' Hershele's blessing, and he, too, would leave money.

R' Hershele did not distribute the money from non-religious Jews, because he was afraid that the money might have been earned on Shabbos. Only in cases of extreme need — for instance, when the one seeking money was on the verge of starvation — did R' Hershele give from this money.

R' Hershele explained his action simply, "*Pikuach nefesh* (the saving of a life) takes precedence over Shabbos."

◆§ Projection

R' Zvi Aryeh Malik used to say, "I despise money, and yet my chassidim persist in giving me large sums. Other rebbes like money, yet their chassidim do not give them much. Why? As I despise money, my chassidim have also learned to despise it. They thus have no hesitation in giving me large donations. On the other hand, those who love money have taught their chassidim to love it as well. As a result, their chassidim are not willing to part with any of it."

◆§ The Full Blessing

A disciple asked R' Avraham of Slonim for a blessing. " 'Hevei Gevir — May you be wealthy,' " said R' Avraham, "but always remember the next word of the verse, 'le'achecha — to your brothers.' Money is only a blessing if it is used to help those in need."

◆§ Too Much Enjoyment

R' Chaim of Brisk used to say, "Both the baal habayis and the cat seek to eliminate any mice in the house, but there is a vast difference between them. The human wants to get rid of all mice forever; the cat wants only to eat a specific mouse now, with the hope of finding another mouse later. By the same token, there are two different ways to give tzedakah — in order to eliminate another's need or, on the other hand, for one's own gratification. There are some people who receive such enjoyment in giving tzedakah that they would be devastated if poverty were totally eliminated."

◆§ To Whom Tzedakah Is Given

Kli Yakar, in his commentary on the Chumash, defines those who are not worthy of tzedakah: "There are, unfortunately, among us those who place a burden upon the community, and are not willing to do any work, even though they are capable of doing so. They complain bitterly if they are not given enough to live on. The Torah commandment of 'You shall help along *with* him,' however, only applies to a person who does whatever he is capable of doing, but nevertheless finds it impossible to support his family. On the other hand, one who simply doesn't want to work, and from the start plans to live on donations — to him we apply the verse, 'You shall refrain from helping him' " (*Shemos* 23:5).

৵ *True Tzedakah*

A person sitting *shivah* for a deceased relative is forbidden to work throughout that entire week. For a poor person this can create real financial hardship. In Frankfurt-am-Main the community had a remarkable way of solving this problem. Whenever a person sat *shivah*, a charity box belonging to the community was placed in his home. This box had a sizable amount of money already in it. If the person was well-to-do, he would add money to what was already there, as would those who came to pay a *shivah* call. If, on the other hand, the person needed money to tide him over during that week, he was permitted to take as much as he needed, without anyone being aware who had given or taken from the box.

৵ *To Whom Were Chazal Referring*

R' Simchah Bunim of Pshischa remarked: "When *Chazal* state that it is irrelevant how much a person gives, provided that whatever he gives is for the sake of Heaven, they were not talking about a poor person. A poor person has to scrape together his pennies in order to give *tzedakah*, and whatever he gives is surely for the sake of Heaven. Therefore, *Chazal* were obviously referring to a wealthy person. They are teaching us that even a wealthy person who gives a great deal of *tzedakah* must do so for the sake of Heaven."

←§ Priorities

R' Levi Yitzchak of Berdichev once approached a certain rabbi and asked him to accompany him while they made the rounds collecting money for a family in very great distress.

"Could you wait for just a few minutes," asked the rabbi, "so I can complete my regular daily quota of *Tehillim*?"

"Please leave what you're doing and come with me immediately," said R' Levi Yitzchak. "Hashem has tens of thousands of angels who will sing His praises even if you don't do so this instant, while this poor man and his family are in immediate danger of drowning in their troubles."

←§ Survival

An old woman used to go around collecting money for the Chevron Yeshiva. Every week, she would faithfully bring whatever she had managed to raise to the *rosh yeshiva,* R' Yechezkel Sarna. The sum never amounted to much.

One of his students once asked R' Yechezkel, "Can the yeshiva survive from such donations?"

"No," replied R' Yechezkel, "the yeshivah cannot survive from such donations, but the *world* can."

←§ No Exemption

R' Menachem of Nivitz, a very wealthy resident of Moscow, was renowned for his generosity to the poor. He imported his own *melamed*, R' Nassan, to teach his children. R' Nassan, a fiery chassid, always went about preaching the importance of *mesiras nefesh* — total dedication to Hashem. One day, the two were together, and R' Nassan said to his employer: "R' Menachem, don't think that by giving large amounts of *tzedakah* you are exempted from praying properly or from setting aside fixed times for Torah. The two realms are separate from one another. Your excuse for not studying has always been that you don't have enough time to do so. Tell me, do you have enough time to sleep? Do you have enough time to eat? If a profitable business deal comes along, do you have time? How is it, then, that the only things you don't have time for are prayer with concentration and Torah study?"

~§ Give Away Five

Each week, R' Shlomo Zalman, the author of *Chemdas Shlomo*, would not bring home the shirt he had taken with him to the bathhouse on Friday, but gave it to a poor man.

Once, he saw six shirts hanging on the clothesline of one of the local homes. He entered the home and said, "I don't see why anyone needs six shirts. Why don't you give away five to those who don't even have one?"

~§ To Prevent Embarrassment

When R' Shlomo Zalman served as *rav* of Warsaw, there were many poor families whom he supported by weekly financial allocations.

A thief was once caught in his home, and it was found that the thief was one of the poor people that R' Shlomo Zalman was supporting.

From that day on, R' Shlomo Zalman would send the weekly allocation to the man's home. He did not want the erstwhile thief to be embarrassed by their meeting.

~§ That Too Is Part of Tzedakah

A poor man, who acted as if he was a prominent rabbi, came to R' Menachem Mendel of Kotzk. R' Menachem Mendel treated him with great respect, arranged a festive meal for him, just as if he was a prominent rabbi. The chassidim who were present found this surprising. After the man had left, one of them asked R' Menachem Mendel, "Rebbe, why did you treat that common person with such respect? Is it because he considers himself a rabbi?"

"It is all part of *tzedakah*," said R' Menachem Mendel. "After all, our Sages tell us that in supplying 'that which he lacks,' one must even give the person a horse to ride on and a servant to run before him. Now, one can understand giving a poor man a horse to ride on, because even a poor person needs to get about. But a servant to run before the person is nothing but a matter of conceit. This shows us that we should support the poor even by catering to their conceits."

৶ We Will Have to Rely Only on Hashem

R' Yosef Yozl of Novarodok took very little from the income of his yeshiva for his personal needs and was always very careful with money.

He was once unsuccessful in persuading a wealthy man to give to the yeshiva. After the conclusion of their talk, R' Yosef Yozl asked that a horse and a wagon be ordered to bring him back home.

"Rebbe," the wealthy man said, "I thought you always walk everywhere to save money."

"Until now, we relied on your support, and I therefore felt that it was my duty to spend as little as possible," said R' Yosef Yozl. "Now, we no longer rely on you, but on Hashem. His hand is open and overflowing. Why should I try to save money?"

৶ Ransom Will Have to Be Paid One Way or Another

R' Hillel of Amshislav came to a wealthy man who was very miserly to ask him to contribute toward the ransoming of captives. The man refused to donate anything.

Some time later, the man's cow broke through his fence and entered the property of his neighbor, a peasant, where it caused extensive damage. The peasant refused to release the cow until the damages had been paid.

When R' Hillel heard of this, he said laughingly, "One who is worthy ransoms Jews who have been taken captive, while one who is not worthy ransoms cows."

Proper Use of Speech

◆§ A Man of Truth

R' David of Bichov was falsely accused and arrested in St. Petersburg. He was brought before a panel of judges for questioning. At one point, the judges wished to consult among themselves, and in order not to be understood, they switched from Russian to French.

R' David, who had been standing at attention throughout the examination, suddenly tilted his head away from the judges. "Prisoner," shouted one of the judges, "when you are before us, you are to remain at attention."

"Your honor," replied R' David, "I heard you speaking French because you didn't want me to hear what you were saying. I know French, however, and I moved my head away so that I would not hear you."

This unexpected reply so staggered the judges that they released R' David immediately.

◈ Entering Into the Heart

Chazal tell us that "words which come from one's heart enter the heart." R' Menachem Mendel of Kotzk explained this, as follows: If what one says comes from his heart and enters his *own* heart, then his words will be able to influence others as well.

◈ Even for a Sigh

A man came to the *Chafetz Chaim* and asked to buy everything the *Chafetz Chaim* had written — except for his *Shemiras HaLashon* — which deals with the prohibition against speaking *lashon hara*. "I'm a businessman," he explained, "and I simply cannot refrain from hearing or speaking *lashon hara*."

"When I first decided to write this work," said the *Chafetz Chaim*, "I asked R' Yisrael Salanter if I should bother. Would the volume change anyone? 'If by your writing the book, you cause one person to sigh just one time for having spoken *lashon hara*,' said R' Yisrael, 'it will have been well worth writing it.' "

◈ Guard Your Tongue

The *Noda B'Yehudah* was a close personal friend of Emperor Josef I of Austria, who very much enjoyed his brilliant insights. When the *Noda B'Yehudah* died, the emperor summoned his son, and asked him, "Are you as wise as your father?" "No," admitted the *Noda B'Yehudah's* son, "I am much less than he."

"That was not the proper way to answer," said the emperor.

"You should have said that your father was much greater than you. By stating that you are less than your father, you are casting aspersions on that brilliant man."

⇜§ Hashem Won't Make Me a Liar

It was said that if R' Zvi Hirsh of Chortkow blessed some-one, Hashem fulfilled that blessing. He once was asked for an explanation of why Hashem always fulfilled his blessings.

"It's really very simple, and it's certainly no miracle," replied R' Zvi Hirsh. "All my life I have made sure never to say anything unnecessary and to always speak the absolute truth. After all my efforts to always tell the truth, would Hashem make me a liar by not granting one of my blessings?"

⇜§ He Is Everywhere

As is known, R' Levi Yitzchak of Berdichev often "argued" with Hashem over the punishments inflicted upon the Jewish people. He was once asked, "The way you talk about Hashem, aren't you guilty of *lashon hara* toward Him?"

"There is a rule," replied R' Levi Yitzchak, "that one does not transgress the laws governing slander if one speaks in front of the person about whom he is talking. Since Hashem is everywhere and hears everything, it isn't slander."

⇜§ Honesty Is the Best Policy

A dead body was found in the town in which the author of the *Machatzis HaShekel* was the *rav*. The deceased had been stabbed to death, and next to the body lay a knife — one which appeared to have come from the *rav's* kitchen. The Jews of the town understood that this was a deliberate attempt to "frame" the *rav*, for there had indeed been a robbery in his house and this knife had been stolen.

His friends suggested that he deny that the knife was from his kitchen, but he refused to follow their advice. When called for questioning he freely admitted the knife was his while denying any connection to the crime. The judges were so impressed with his honesty that he was immediately released.

Later he explained why he had insisted on telling the truth: "I emulated the actions of Yehudah, when he was sent by Yosef to bring back his brother Binyamin. Yehudah could have assumed that the Egyptian ruler would not know the difference and brought back any other man of the same age. But he insisted on bringing back Binyamin himself because his conscience would not allow him to do otherwise. By the same token," the *rav* concluded, "I simply am unable to let a falsehood pass my lips, regardless of the possible consequences."

⋅§ How to Address People

The *Chafetz Chaim* was very insistent that the sermons of itinerant *maggidim* should not emphasize the punishment involved for sinning. Instead, he would have them stress the importance and beauty of the *mitzvos*, along with the bounty from Hashem for those who obey them. "The Jews of our times," he would say, "are so oppressed and persecuted, suffer such great want, and find their suffering increasing so intensely from day to day that there is no reason to add more woes to those which they are already suffering."

⋅§ I Meant Every Word

When R' Nachum was the *rav* of Horodna, the non-Jewish governor was a notorious anti-Semite, who sought to harm the Jews wherever possible. The only Jew whom he respected was R' Nachum because of his reputation as a *tzaddik* and for never lying.

On January 1, the Jewish leaders would visit the governor to wish him a happy new year. One year, the governor accepted their greetings and dismissed them. Only R'

Nachum was asked to remain behind.

"Rabbi," said the governor, "I'm no fool. I know exactly what the Jews think of me, and I even know why. I'm sure that they're upset with me for all types of reasons. I also understand that they come to wish me a happy new year as a common courtesy, even though none of them means a word. What surprises me is that you come too. After all, you are known as a truthful man, so how could you come to wish me a happy new year?"

"Your excellency," replied R' Nachum, "we meant every word we said. We wished you a happy new year. Now what would you consider to be a happy new year? No doubt, the best thing that could happen to you would be to be promoted. Then you would leave Horodna. And that is something that every Jew in Horodna wishes you."

⋅§ It's Not His Fault

R' Levi Yitzchak of Berdichev once entered a *shul* and heard an itinerant *maggid* addressing the people. In his speech, the *maggid* breathed fire and brimstone, castigating the people for all types of sins, both sins between man and Hashem and sins between man and man.

Finally, when the *maggid* had finished, R' Levi Yitzchak raised his voice in prayer: "Hashem," he said, "the *maggid* surely didn't mean what he said about Your people. He no doubt has a daughter of marriageable age whose wedding he must now arrange. To raise money for this, he goes from town to town and speaks. Grant him, I pray You, enough money to marry his daughter, so that he will not have to continue to malign Your children."

⋅§ No Lashon Hara, Please!

R' Rafael of Hamburg left his position as *rav* of the city because of the exposure to *lashon hara* the job entailed. He nevertheless remained good friends with a number of his former congregants. When they would visit him, he would tell them, "Please, let's not talk about anyone except you and me."

⌁§ The Absolute Truth

R' Pinchas of Koretz was known for his devotion to speaking only the truth. Once he met R' Nachum of Chernobyl, who asked him, "R' Pinchas, I know that you are scrupulous in your devotion to the truth. But what do you do when two people have quarreled and you wish to bring them back together?"

"In such a case, said R' Pinchas, "I make sure that whatever I say is *absolutely* true, and that way I get the two people to become friends again."

⌁§ The Middle Ground

Once, the *Malbim* was in Berlin and happened to hear a particular *maskil* preach. Unfortunately, the rabbi's words were void of any real message, and the *Malbim* felt that he had wasted his time. Later, however, he stated that he had indeed learned something from the speech. "*Koheles*," he said, "gives us no less than twenty-eight contrasts, such as 'a time to love and a time to hate,' or 'a time to weep and a time to laugh.' In all of these contrasts, there is a middle ground. After all, one can be in a state where he neither loves nor hates, or when he is neither weeping nor crying. There is one contrast in *Koheles*, though, that always puzzled me. That is the one which states, 'a time to talk and a time to remain silent.' Up to now, I could not understand where the middle ground between the two could be. After having heard this speaker, however, I see that it is possible for a person not to remain silent and yet say nothing!" People understood that this *maskil* was someone whose speeches should not be attended.

✒ The Proper Way to Offer Rebuke

R' Aryeh Levin once saw a number of people lined up in front of a small ice cream store in Jerusalem just before Shabbos. He realized that the only way all the people could be served would be if the storekeeper kept his store open into Shabbos. On the other hand, R' Aryeh realized what a temptation it must be to the storekeeper. After thinking a moment, R' Aryeh pushed his way into the line, approached the storekeeper and said to him, "Dear Jew, I know what a temptation you are facing right now, but it is almost Shabbos, and we are commanded to observe it." Before the man had a chance to say a word, R' Aryeh had run off.

On Sunday, the storekeeper came over to R' Aryeh and told him, "Rabbi, you were so kind and tactful in your words that I was able to withstand the temptation and closed my store immediately."

✒ The Truth Regardless

R' Yaakov Yitzchak, the *Chozeh* of Lublin, had many chassidim, but felt unworthy of being a Rebbe. He implored people not to come to him, but to no avail. Finally, he approached R' Ezriel, the rabbi of Lublin, and asked him what he should do.

"My advice to you is simple," replied R' Ezriel. "On the next *Yom Tov*, when all your chassidim are gathered about you, tell them that you are ignorant in Torah and lacking in good deeds, and that you are not worthy of their adulation."

The *Chozeh* did as R' Ezriel had advised him, but the effect was exactly the opposite. Everyone talked about how humble he was, and the next *Yom Tov* an even greater number of chassidim came to him.

The *Chozeh* returned to R' Ezriel and described what had happened. "Well then," said R' Ezriel, "at the next *Yom Tov*, why don't you tell everyone what a great Torah scholar and *tzaddik* you are? That way, all will think you are conceited and stop coming to you."

"Heaven forbid," said the *Chozeh*. "I may be ignorant and lacking in good deeds, and indeed am unworthy of having people come to me, but I am not willing to lie!"

◄§ To Know What Not to Say

A certain great Torah genius was reputed to be as brilliant as R' Chaim Brisker, and, in fact, often came up with the same brilliant insights in Torah as R' Chaim. This *talmid chacham*, however, never attained the prominence of R' Chaim. When asked why this was so, R' Boruch Ber Leibowitz explained, "R' Chaim had one tremendous advantage over the other *talmid chacham*. Not only did he know what to say, he also knew what *not* to say."

◄§ You Hear What You Want to

When all his chassidim would push forward to hear him speak, R' Avraham Yehoshua Heshel of Apta would say: "It doesn't pay for you to push forward. One who is able to hear will hear even if he is standing from far away, while one who is not able to hear will not hear even if he is standing right next to me."

Family Life

Marriage

⋖§ A Strong Defense

The wife of R' Levi Yitzchak of Berdichev once brought him to a *beis din*. "My husband," she complained, "has not fulfilled the conditions of the *kesubah* (marriage contract). The *kesubah* states clearly that he must feed and clothe me, 'as is the custom of Jewish men,' but the amount of money he earns is simply not enough to meet his obligation."

"My wife is absolutely right," said R' Levi Yitzchak. "But immediately afterwards in the *kesubah*, it states '. . .the way Jewish men support their wives *honestly*.' To earn money honestly, without cheating or taking advantage of anyone, is, unfortunately, very difficult."

✑ Priorities

The *Chafetz Chaim* was once together with his rebbe, R'
Nachum of Horodna, on a Chanukah night. Night fell, but R'
Nachum did not light the Chanukah candles. It grew later and
later, and R' Nachum still did not light.

Hours after the prescribed time for lighting, R' Nachum's
wife entered. Only then did R' Nachum light the candles.

Later, the *Chafetz Chaim* asked R' Nachum why he had
delayed lighting the candles. After all, the *halachah* is that a
husband can light the candles on behalf of his wife even if she
is not physically present.

"The reason," said R' Nachum, "is that my wife works very
hard to support our family and enable me to study Torah. She
loves seeing the candles being lit, and I felt that *shalom bayis*
— marital harmony — required me to wait for her to return
home to light the candles."

✑ The Value of a Wife

R' David of Zavlatov became deathly ill. The doctors
attending him were helpless and announced that death was
imminent. But R' David's wife, Pesia Leah, refused to accept
their verdict. She kept reciting *Tehillim* and prayers at her
husband's bedside for weeks on end, until he finally recovered.

After he had fully recovered, R' David remarked, "Now I
understand why the *Midrash* says that Nadav and Avihu died
because they didn't have wives. Had they had wives like my
Pesia Leah, their wives would certainly have saved them from
death."

✑ Whose Choice?

A chassid complained to R' Moshe of Kobrin that his
daughter refused to marry the young man he had chosen for

her. "You have no cause to complain," said R' Moshe. "Did Hashem not tell Moshe that the daughters of Tzelafchad should marry 'those who appeal to them'? The groom must appeal to the bride, not to her father."

✥ Thirty Days' Grace

R' Shmuel Salanter always did everything he could to convince couples to reconcile without divorce. Once, however, a couple came to him, and both were adamant that they wished to be divorced. Nothing R' Shmuel said could persuade them differently. Finally, R' Shmuel agreed to arrange the divorce. Of course, the first thing he needed to know was the name of the wife. "My name is Ratchke," the woman said.

"That's a very strange name," said R' Shmuel, "one I've never heard before."

"Well, actually," the woman said, "my name is Raizie, but people gradually starting calling me Ratchke, and the name stuck."

"That presents us with a real problem as to what to write in the *get* (bill of divorce)," said R' Shmuel. "Therefore, you should return home and be sure that for the next thirty days no one calls you by the name Ratchke. You are to be called Raizie and nothing else."

The couple returned home, and during those thirty days they were reconciled and never returned to complete the divorce proceedings.

✥ Gold-Plated Fraud

R' Pinchas of Koretz once returned home and found a new gold goblet. He criticized his wife for having introduced such luxuries into the house and expressed his fear that such signs of material wealth could lead to pride. Nor was he mollified when his wife told him that the goblet was only gold plated.

"That makes it doubly bad," said R' Pinchas. "Not only does it introduce pride into the house but falsehood as well."

◆§ Sorry, She's Married!

A great *talmid chacham* lost his wife and wished to remarry. His grown children, however, were opposed to his remarrying. One of them mentioned another *talmid chacham* who had recently lost his wife and had expressed his intention not to remarry because he was married to the Torah.

"That settles it then," said the father. "I will have to look for a wife after all, especially as you have told me that the Torah is already a married woman!"

Parents and Children

⋗ Like a Tree

R' Uri of Strelisk used to say: "Man is like a tree. Just as one cannot stand staring at a tree to watch it grow, so one cannot keep a child under constant supervision. If one takes care of the tree properly — watering it, adding fertilizer, pruning and weeding it — the tree will grow by itself. So, too, must one ensure that the proper atmosphere is available to a child, so that he will mature properly on his own."

⋗ Not by Itself

A man once asked the *Chafetz Chaim* for a blessing that his children grow up to become pious Jews. "That," the *Chafetz Chaim* replied, "requires more than a blessing. It requires much effort and dedication on your part!"

ᴥᴈ Notice the Limp

R' Meir Shapiro of Lublin rebuked a young man for not emulating his father, a great *talmid chacham* and *tzaddik*.

"How can you say that I am not like my father?" replied the young man. "Doesn't the *Gemara* describe a son as 'the leg of his father,' meaning that he is like his father?"

"Now that you mention it," said R' Meir, "I remember that your father had a noticeable limp."

ᴥᴈ Respect for One's Father

The *Chiddushei HaRim* used to give a *shiur* to some outstanding young men, including his son R' Avraham Mordechai.

After a *shiur* devoted to a particularly difficult topic, the students told the *Chiddushei HaRim* that they had not understood the *shiur*. The *Chiddushei HaRim* turned to his son in frustration and asked, "You didn't understand the *shiur* either?" R' Avraham Mordechai replied that he had not.

The *Chiddushei HaRim* then left the room. When he returned, he found his son explaining the *shiur* to the other students. The *Chiddushei HaRim* asked his son why he had told him that he did not understand the *shiur*.

R' Avraham Mordechai replied, "Father, if you had asked me whether I understood the *shiur,* I would have said, 'Yes'. But you asked, 'You didn't understand the *shiur* either?' and I did not wish to contradict you."

ᴥᴈ Respect for Torah Scholars

R' Chaim Soloveitchik used to stand out of respect every time his son, R' Velvele, entered the room. To avoid this, R' Velvele began entering their home by climbing through the window.

⋙ Ask the Proper Person

A distinguished chassid once came to R' Zvi Hirsh, the son of the Baal Shem Tov, and begged him to teach him how to become a *tzaddik*.

Reb Zvi Hirsch replied with a story: "There were two very wealthy men in a certain town. One had inherited an enormous fortune from his father, while the other had become wealthy by dint of his own efforts. A man once asked the first to teach him how to become rich. 'I can't,' he explained. 'I inherited all my wealth. Go to the one who earned all his money if you want to know how to become rich.'

"The same is true of me," said R' Zvi Hirsh. "Whatever I have, I inherited from my father, and there is nothing I can teach you. If you wish to become a *tzaddik*, go to R' Aharon of Karlin. He was a simple man but made himself into a *tzaddik*."

⋙ Greater Yichus

R' Naftali of Ropshitz was speaking to his chassidim about all his illustrious forebears. One of the chassidim told him: "Rebbe, my *yichus* (lineage) is greater than yours. Of my entire family, I am the only one who puts on *tefillin* and washes his hands before eating bread." R' Naftali chuckled and told him, "You are correct. Your stature is more important than that of your ancestors."

⋙ It's All in the Mind

When R' Chaim of Brisk was eight years old, his father, the *Beis Halevi,* said to him, "Chaimke, the *Gemara* tells us that Hashem considers our intention to do a good deed as if we already did it. Right now, I'm thinking of a very hard question, so it is as if I already asked it. Can you answer it?"

Without hesitating, the little boy answered, "Father, I'm thinking of a very good answer. Can you refute it?"

✑ Treat Your Children as I Treat Mine

The author of *Be'er Mayim Chaim* had a son who threw off the yoke of the Torah. His father did not banish him, but continued to supply him with all his wants. From time to time, he would lift his eyes to the heavens and pray, "Hashem, please treat Your children the way I treat mine. I, too, have a child who left the proper path, but I still love him and give him whatever he needs."

✑ Why Is Israel Unique?

R' Meir Simchah of Dvinsk explained: "Just as the firstborn receives a double inheritance because it is he who made his father into a father, so too, did the Jewish people which made Hashem into our Father when we chose Him and accepted Him."

✑ You Have No Problem

R' Baruch of Sanz came to his father, R' Chaim, and told him that he was in dire need of money, for he had a daughter to be married right then and did not have the money for the wedding and dowry.

As they finished speaking, a few rich chassidim came in to R' Chaim, and after receiving his blessing left him a sizable amount of money as a donation. R' Chaim immediately called his *shamash* and had him summon a poor man who was waiting outside. Handing him all the money, R' Chaim told the poor man, "With this amount you should be able to marry off your daughter."

After the poor man had left, R' Baruch asked his father, "Why did you give the money to that man, when I, too, need money for my daughter's wedding? Am I any less in need than that man?"

"On the contrary," said his father, "the difference is that you can go from place to place and collect money for your daughter's wedding. I am sure that when people find out that you are my son, they will give you freely. On the other hand, if this poor man had gone out to collect money for his daughter, do you think anyone would have paid attention to him?"

◄§ Disqualifying Himself

A father and son once called upon R' Yitzchak Feigenbaum of Warsaw to resolve a legal dispute between them. In the course of presenting their arguments, the son repeatedly ridiculed his father. Finally, R' Yitzchak rose and declared that he was disqualifying himself from ruling. The son's treatment of his father, he explained, caused him to hate the son and thus rendered him incapable of judging the case.

◄§ Proper Perspective

When the financial situation in the home of the *Chafetz Chaim* reached a new low and the family suffered greatly, his wife blurted out, "Why is our situation so desperate, when that of our neighbors, who are simple folk, is so much better?"

"Do you really think that there is injustice in the world?" asked the *Chafetz Chaim.* "Look at our children, and think how much *nachas* we have watching them grow up as fine Torah Jews. Unfortunately, our neighbors' children do not give them that much *nachas*, so Hashem had to find a way to reward them monetarily."

◄§ A Baker's Wisdom

The parents of the Rebbe of Ostrovtze were simple folk, his father earning his living as a baker. The Rebbe was once sitting among other *rabbanim*. Each one repeated a Torah thought he had heard from his father. When it came time for the Rebbe to speak, he said, "My father, of blessed memory, used to say that a freshly baked item is better than one which is rewarmed and stale."

◄§ That's the Tragedy

In his old age, the *Chasam Sofer's* eyesight failed him. His son read him the hundreds of *shaylos* sent to him from around the world each week, and he would dictate his answers.

One such letter was replete with phrases praising the *Chasam Sofer* as the "light of the generation," etc. As the *Chasam Sofer* heard all the titles bestowed upon him, he uttered a deep sigh.

"Father, why are you sighing?" asked his son. "After all, you are considered by everyone to be the greatest *talmid chacham* of our generation."

"That's exactly why I'm sighing," said the *Chasam Sofer*. "I cannot help thinking how poor is a generation in which I am considered the greatest *talmid chacham*."

◄§ A Common Language Between the Generations

"Some people," said the *Chafetz Chaim*, "think that all they have to do is send their sons to yeshiva, but they themselves need not learn. When the sons return from the yeshiva, they have nothing to talk about with their fathers. That is why, the Torah stresses, 'You shall teach them to your sons to speak of them' (*Devarim* 11:19) — even if you are busy with your daily cares you should continue to have a fixed time for Torah study. Only then will you have a common language with your sons."

 Illness

≈§ A Cure for Illness

A man who was seriously ill asked R' Yechiel Michel of Gustinin to pray that he be cured. R' Yechiel Michel told him instead to recite *Tehillim*. "But Rebbe," protested the man, "I don't even understand the words."

R' Yechiel Michel opened the *Tehillim* to chapter 6 and said: "Here we are told that King David played a *sheminis*, a harp with eight strings. Other harps have only four strings. There is also a music box where one produces the music by turning a handle.

"The common element is that some type of human action is necessary to produce the music. The same is true of praying to Hashem. One cannot rely on someone else; one must pray oneself. Even a person who doesn't understand the meaning of the words must recite *Tehillim* himself."

◄§ A Truthful Answer

R' Leib Chasid of Kelm once replied to a friend who asked how he was feeling after a serious illness: "Thank God, a little worse."

◄§ An Orderly Progression

R' Chaim David of Pietrkov was both a renowned *tzaddik* and a famed doctor. The proper approach to treating the sick, he said, is outlined in the *yotzer hame'oros* blessing before the morning *Shema*. Hashem is described successively as: "*Borei refu'os* (Creator of cures), *Nora tehillos* (too awesome for praise), *Adon ha'nifla'os* (Lord of wonders)." The first step is to give the patient medicine (*Brei refu'os*). If that doesn't help, one must recite *Tehillim* (*Nora tehillos*). And if even that does not cure the patient, one must hope for a miracle (*Adon ha'nifla'os*).

◄§ Hashem's Desire Is What Counts

R' Yisrael Salanter once became very ill. After one of his examinations, the doctor told R' Yisrael's family that he had improved somewhat. When R' Yisrael overheard this, he exclaimed, "What do I care if I'm in better health or not? All I want is what Hashem wants of me."

◄§ How Is the Child?

A young married man came to Rabbi Yaakov Kaminetzky one Shabbos to asked what he could do for his sick child on Shabbos. R' Yaakov told him precisely what to do, and the young man left. Some time later, there was a knock on the young man's door. R' Yaakov, then over eighty years old, stood at the door. "How is the child?" he wanted to know.

✺§ No Need for Bars

The *Chafetz Chaim* once visited a sick Jew. On the way, he observed: "When a king wishes to restrict a person's movements, he builds a prison, places a high wall around it, and then posts guards in towers all along the walls. Hashem, however, doesn't need any walls or guards. If He wants to restrict a person's movements, He simply afflicts him with an illness so that he cannot get up from his bed."

✺§ The Cure, Not the Cause

R' Moshe Feinstein was sleeping when someone knocked at the door. His wife knew that the gravely ill *gadol* desperately needed more sleep and ignored the knocking. R' Moshe, however, awakened and asked his wife to open the door. When she demurred, he told her. "You don't understand. Visitors make me feel better. I derive my strength from them."

✺§ There Will Be Time to Sleep

R' Baruch of Medzhibozh became very ill and his doctors prescribed that he sleep more each night. R' Baruch, however, rejected the advice. "If I sleep in this world, what will I do in the grave?" he asked.

✺§ True Appreciation

A woman came crying to R' Baruch Ber Leibowitz. Her daughter was in the midst of a difficult labor, and both mother and child were in great danger. The woman begged R' Baruch Ber to pray for her daughter, and he immediately dropped what he was doing and prayed with great emotion for the daughter's welfare.

As the woman was about to leave, she handed R' Baruch Ber a piece of newspaper with some coins in it. R' Baruch Ber unwrapped the newspaper and saw that the amount inside was a pittance — barely enough to buy bread. He immediately called to his son-in-law, R' Reuven Grozovsky, and in the woman's presence, exclaimed, "Reuven, please come here. We have a donation for the yeshiva!"

✑ Visiting the Sick

R' Shimon Sofer of Cracow vacationed one year in Marienbad, and while there he became ill. R' Shimon Wolf Rothschild, a pious member of the Rothschild family, was also in Marienbad at the time. He visited R' Shimon Sofer, but remained for only a short time. Asked why his guest had remained so short a time, R' Shimon answered, "We deduce the obligation to visit the sick from the verse, 'the way in which they will go.' From this it follows that when a person visits someone who is sick, he must do so in accordance with 'they will go,' and not stay too long and thereby cause the sick person any discomfort or distress."

✑ You Have to Be Different

R' Yospe of Ostraha was a very wealthy man. When his daughter became very ill, he distributed tzedakah to different people, asking only that they pray for his daughter's recovery. Many of those who had received the tzedakah from R' Yospe embarked on a series of fasts, begging Hashem to save the girl.

One of those who was given tzedakah to pray for the girl was the saintly R' Yitzchak of Drohowitz. R' Yitzchak, unlike the others who had received money to pray for the girl, used the money to buy a feast, which he ate.

Later, after the girl had recovered, some of R' Yitzchak's friends asked him, "Rebbe, why didn't you act like the others and embark on a fast?" R' Yitzchak explained to them, "If I had fasted, that would have made absolutely no impression in Heaven. They're used to my fasting for days on end, and another fast would have been of no consequence. However, when I used the money to prepare a lavish feast, they immediately took notice in Heaven and asked, 'Why is it that R' Yitzchak is suddenly eating a full meal? Where did he get the money?' They began to investigate what had happened, and soon found out that R' Yospe's daughter had become ill, and her father had given lots of *tzedakah*. It was then that they sent her a cure."

◀§ *Having Time*

A man once approached R' Avraham Mordechai of Gur when the latter was in a great hurry. He thrust a note into the Rebbe's hand and awaited his blessing.

"I am really very sorry," said R' Avraham Mordechai, "but I don't have the time to read this right now."

"I have had the time to take care of my sick daughter for the past twenty years, and the Rebbe doesn't have a moment for her?" the man said.

R' Avraham Mordechai immediately read the note and stopped all he was doing to pray for the man's daughter.

Death and Dying

◆§ A Father's Advice

In his youth, R' Avraham Mordechai of Gur was once gravely ill. The doctors had given up all hope, and R' Avraham Mordechai's spirits were very low. His father, the *Chiddushei HaRim*, approached his bed and whispered to him, "Know, my son, that it is a *mitzvah* to want to live." He added his own prayer that his son recover and produce a worthy son.

R' Avraham Mordechai did indeed recover and have a son. That son was the *Sefas Emes*.

◆§ A Funeral Oration

The *Chafetz Chaim* recounted at the funeral of one of his sons the story of a woman whose two sons were killed before her very eyes during the Spanish Inquisition. She lifted her eyes to Heaven and whispered, "Hashem, I confess that while my sons were alive, my love of You was not complete; I left a corner in my heart for the love of my sons. Now that my sons are dead, all of my love is only for You, and I can completely fulfill the *mitzvah* of loving You with all my heart."

When he had finished the story, the *Chafetz Chaim* concluded, "The love which I had for my son until now I hereby offer to You."

◈ Only You

Soon after losing his wife, R' Menachem Mendel of Rimanov lost his daughter as well. He learned of his daughter's passing just prior to the *Mussaf* service on Shabbos and exclaimed, "Hashem, when my wife died, I still had my beloved daughter in whom to rejoice. Now that You have taken her as well, I only have You with Whom to rejoice."

◈ A Nicer Dwelling

R' Menachem Mendel of Kotzk used to say, "Dying is no different than moving from one room to another. The wise man, however, makes every effort to ensure that he receives a nicer room than the one he currently occupies."

◈ A True Confession

As R' Michel of Zlotchov lay on his deathbed, his disciple, R' Aharon Leib Yechiel of Premishlan, suggested he recite the deathbed *vidui* (confession). R' Michel Yechiel immediately began his *vidui*: "Hashem, I hereby confess, as I am preparing to leave the world, that I have fulfilled all the *mitzvos* of the Torah to the best of my ability. I have never transgressed against Your will in thought or in deed."

Those present were astonished because the *vidui* is generally a recital of one's sins. Later, R' Aharon Leib explained to them the source of his Rebbe's *vidui*. "*Vidui* is found in only one place in the Torah. In the third and sixth years of the *Shmittah* cycle, after the separation of the tithes, one recites the *vidui ma'aser*. Included in that *vidui* is the statement: 'I have not violated your commandment and have forgotten nothing . . . I have obeyed [You], G-d my Lord, and have done all that You commanded me.' Fortunate is the man who is able to recite such a *vidui* on his deathbed."

৶ How Not to Fear Death

A man confessed to R' Hillel of Radoshitz that he was afraid of dying. "If you live with the fear of sin," the Rebbe replied, "you have nothing to fear from death."

৶ How to Draw up a Will

A man once asked the *Chafetz Chaim* for advice in formulating a will. He showed the *Chafetz Chaim* his proposed will in which he bequeathed everything to his wife and three sons.

"You've overlooked a very important beneficiary," the *Chafetz Chaim* told him. In response to his look of puzzlement, the *Chafetz Chaim* explained, "You have violated the commandment, 'You shall not ignore your own flesh,' which refers to oneself as well as one's family, since a man is closest to himself. Your will makes no provision for *tzedakah*. Doesn't your own soul deserve something in your will?"

৶ Maybe R' Meir?

As R' Yonasan Eybeschuetz lay dying, the community leaders of Altona-Hamburg, where he was the *rav*, gathered around his bedside and asked him who should replace him. R' Yonasan whispered, "Maybe R' Meir?"

After R' Yonasan's funeral, the community leaders began looking for a new *rav*. Many distinguished *rabbanim* were interested in the post, but none by the name of R' Meir. The community leaders decided, at last, that the position would be filled by the candidate who was able to explain R' Yonasan's dying words. A number of suggestions were advanced, but none satisfied the communal leaders.

Finally, R' Yitzchak Horowitz of Brody was invited to meet the communal leaders and asked to explain R' Yonasan's last words. "It is really quite simple," he said. "R' Yonasan was not referring to any individual named R' Meir. He was telling you that your presumption that he would not recover was premature, and thus your question about his successor was improper. It was R' Meir in the *Gemara* who always required that one take into account even a slight possibility and not just rely on the principle of majority. R' Yonasan meant that the *halachah* might be in accord with R' Meir, and you should take into account the slight possibility that he would recover."

R' Yitzchak was thereupon appointed to succeed R' Yonasan.

◈§ My Tallis as Witness

R' David ben Shmuel Halevi, known as the *Taz*, was the *rav* of Lwow for the last thirteen years of his life. The pious women of the city noticed that his *tallis* was old and frayed, and they collected money and bought him a beautiful new *tallis*. R' David, though, refused to accept the gift. "I am very grateful to you," he told the women, "but I wish to pray in my old *tallis* for the rest of my days, for it will testify in the World-to-Come that I never had any improper thoughts during *Shemoneh Esrei*."

◈§ Nothing to Fear

As R' Yisrael Salanter lay close to death, he explained to the man attending him that there is no reason to fear a dead body. That same day R' Yisrael died with only his attendant present. Even as he sensed that his time had come, R' Yisrael's greatest concern was that his attendant should not be frightened when it happened.

◄§ The Weeping Tallis

R' Moshe Yitzchak, the *Maggid* of Kelm, once came to a resort town near Riga. When he went to *daven*, he noticed that many of the men there were not wearing *talleisim*. They had simply not bothered to pack *talleisim* for their vacations.

That Shabbos afternoon R' Moshe Yitzchak was called upon to speak. "My friends," he began, "rather than give a lecture, I would like to tell you a story. Some time ago, I went to visit someone. He was not home, but from inside the house I heard weeping. Upon closer inspection, I found his *tallis* sobbing that its master had left it behind when he went on vacation. Only his gold and silver had been taken along. 'Don't worry, *tallis*,' I said. 'There will come a time in the not-too-distant future when your master will go on a much longer journey. Then he will leave all his gold and silver behind and take only you with him.' "

◄§ To the Very End

An old Kotzker chassid was dying. At his side was R' Wolf of Strikov. R' Wolf bent down to the dying man and asked him: "Tell me, is the *yetzer hara* still with you even now?"

"Indeed he is," answered the chassid.

"And what does he say?"

"He is trying to persuade me," said the dying man, "to say the *Shema* right now, so that people will say, 'What a *tzaddik*, he died with the word *echad* on his lips.' "

◄§ Whose Duty Is It?

An argument once broke out between the *Chevrah Kadishah* of Kovno and the *Chevrah Kadishah* of Slobodka, a suburb of Kovno, as to who had the responsibility for burying a certain destitute woman. R' Yisrael Salanter overheard the argument while he was in the middle of *Shacharis*. He immediately removed his *tefillin* and told his *talmidim* to come with him, explaining that the old woman was in the category of a *meis mitzvah*, a person who has no one to bury him or her. Reb Yisrael told his students that the *mitzvah* to bury her is incumbent on everyone and takes precedence over anything else one might be doing.

⋙ Dying of Pride

A very wealthy man in Vilna lost everything he had. Rather than appeal to others for help, he tried to hide his situation and eventually died of malnutrition. The people of Vilna were very distressed that a neighbor had starved to death without anyone helping. R' Yisrael Salanter, however, consoled them: "That man did not die of starvation but of excessive pride. Had he been willing to ask others for help and admit to his situation, he would not have died of hunger."

⋙ For Visitors Only

R' Naftali of Ropshitz used to say: "Only once in my life was I bested in conversation. I came to the little village of Zabov, where only ten adult Jewish males lived. Nevertheless, they had both a *shul* and a cemetery. I met a little girl in the street and asked her, if one man of the ten men in town dies and you use the cemetery, you won't need the *shul,* and if you have a *shul* for ten men to pray in, why do you need a cemetery? She answered me on the spot: 'The cemetery is for visitors passing through our village.' "

⋙ The Power of the Dead

R' Hirsch of Volozhin once traveled to a distant health resort in search of a cure to an ailment from which he was suffering. When he attended the local *shul*, he was astonished to see that almost everyone in the *shul* recited *Kaddish*.

Going over to the *shamash* after *davening* he asked, "Was there some type of epidemic here last year that everyone in the *shul* says *Kaddish?*"

"Not at all," replied the *shamash* with a smile, "but in this country most people don't come to *shul* unless they have to say *Kaddish*."

"Now," said R' Hirsch, "I can better understand a verse in *Koheles*, 'I praise more highly the dead who have died than the live ones who are still alive.' While parents who are alive in this city obviously don't have the power to bring their children to *shul*, as soon as they die, they have the power to bring their children to *shul* three times a day."

⤳ *You Can Begin*

When the Nazis came to Kelm, they forced all the Jews to dig their own graves. Once these long trenches had been dug, the Jews were lined up and the machine guns readied. Just then, the *rav* of Kelm, R' Daniel Movshovitz, went over to the Nazi monster in charge and said to him, "I would like just a few moments to speak to the people." Surprisingly, the German agreed, provided that he didn't take long.

The *rav* then began to explain quietly to everyone — as if this was simply another *shiur* — the rules governing dying *al kiddush Hashem*. As the German saw that it was taking too long, he screamed at the *rav* to hurry up and finish. The *rav* then turned to all the Jews and said, "We are now confronted with the situation I have been discussing with you until now — dying *al kiddush Hashem*. Please do not panic. We must quietly accept the verdict." He then addressed the German officer, "I've finished. You can begin."

⋖§ To Live as a Jew

A chassid came to R' Yehoshua of Belz and asked for a blessing that he die a Jew. "There is nothing special about that," said the Rebbe. "Even the wicked Bilaam asked, 'Let my death be the death of the righteous.' The main thing is to live as a Jew."

⋖§ The True Pain

Two days before R' Meir Simchah of Dvinsk died, he was visited by one of his students. Though obviously in very great pain, he was nevertheless learning Torah by heart, reciting it aloud. The student overheard him say, "Hashem, my suffering is so great that I cannot learn Torah properly."

The Community

Communal Life

✑ A Lesson From the Midwives

One of the *Chafetz Chaim*'s best students was offered the post as *rav* of a community. The *talmid* was reluctant to accept the position because of the tremendous responsibility involved. The *Chafetz Chaim* told him, "When the midwives were told to kill the newborn males, they disregarded Pharaoh's explicit orders. Why didn't they simply resign? The reason is that they realized Pharaoh would simply appoint someone else who would obey."

"By the same token," the *Chafetz Chaim* concluded, "if people such as you don't take positions of responsibility, they can be sure that someone else who lacks their sense of responsibility will take them."

❧ Blessing and Curse

When R' Shimon Sofer became the *rav* of Cracow, he found the city splintered into various groups, each with its own *minyan*. In fact, there were well over a hundred *minyanim* in the city. In his very first sermon, he told the community, "We know that Bilaam had no love for the Jewish people, and that anything he said in our praise was not out of any affection for us. Therefore I was always puzzled by his words, 'How goodly are your tents, O Yaakov.' After coming to Cracow, I understand them better. Bilaam saw how many different *shuls* and *batei medrash* there were, how the people were divided up into many different groups, with nothing uniting them. He then 'blessed' the nation that in future they should continue in the same fashion, with all the people divided into different *shuls*. Unfortunately, we still suffer from his 'blessing' today."

❧ Elections, Elections

The *Beis Halevi* was once invited to a certain town which was about to appoint a new *rav*. The town had divided into two camps, each with its own candidate for the post. Matters had gotten so out of hand that the people had literally stopped working at their trades and instead spent their entire time enlisting support for their candidates.

When R' Yosef Ber got up to speak to them, he told them, 'There is a certain passage in the Torah which always puzzled me. We are told than when the people cried to Moshe about the absence of meat to eat, Hashem told him to gather seventy elders. What purpose was served by selecting seventy elders at that time, when all were busy complaining about the lack of food? After having seen what is going on here, I can understand it better.

"When Hashem told Moshe to select seventy elders, He realized that everyone would become so totally engrossed in choosing them that they would completely forget about their lack of food."

← I'm Absolutely Sincere

R' Amram Blum was the *rav* of a town in Hungary. He was constantly trying to inspire the Jews of his town to improve their ways, but he met with scant success. They went on ignoring the commandments, no matter how much he preached.

After some time, R' Amram requested a raise in salary, but the community leaders turned him down. When informed of their decision, R' Amram told the community heads:

"You have no idea how happy you have made me by turning down my request. *Chazal* tell us that words from the heart influence the heart of the listener. All this time, I have been afraid that you weren't listening to me because my pleas lacked sincerity. But when I asked you for a raise — a request from the depths of my heart — and you nevertheless didn't listen to me, I realized the problem is not my lack of sincerity but your hardheartedness."

← Not Letting the Honor Go to One's Eyes

When R' Yehudah Greenwald was appointed the *rav* of Satmar, thousands of people of all ages came out to greet him. As soon as he saw the large crowd, R' Yehudah told his *shamash* to lead him to his house as if he were blind so that he would not derive any pleasure from the sight of the large crowd gathered to honor him.

← Not to Have to Dig It Out

R' Meir Shapiro was once invited to lay the cornerstone for a Talmud Torah in a nearby town. When he arrived, the station was packed with thousands of people who had come to greet him.

R' Meir began his address, "I did not come here for the

honor, but to urge you to complete the building as soon as possible. Today you are honoring me but the honor will only be complete when you finish the building. Please don't make me return after I die to dig up the cornerstone that I am laying today with my bare hands."

⋙ Priorities

One of the students of the *Chafetz Chaim* was invited to become the *rav* of a certain town. Before assuming his post, the young man came to the *Chafetz Chaim* for advice. The *Chafetz Chaim* told him: "The Torah tells us, 'You shall be guiltless before Hashem and Yisrael' (*Bamidbar* 32:22). First a *rav* must be guiltless before Hashem — i.e., he must keep all the *mitzvos*. After that, he must fulfill his obligations to Yisrael — to his community. That is the order of the verse. If a *rav* reverses the order of the verse, and seeks favor in the eyes of the community prior to seeking Hashem's favor, he will fail on both counts."

⋙ Sell the Torah!

R' Yisrael Salanter once rebuked the members of his community for not paying the tuition costs of a certain orphan, who, as a result, idled away his time on the city streets. The community leaders claimed that there was no money available, but R' Yisrael refused to accept their excuses. He told them, "If you need money, sell one of the Torah scrolls and pay for the boy's tuition with it!"

⋙ The Beis Din's Fault

R' Avraham of Strettin used to say: "A *Sanhedrin* that executes someone once in seventy years is called "bloodthirsty," for if its members had been totally righteous, no murders would have taken place in their days."

⋙ Whom to Change

R' Levi Yitzchak of Berdichev used to say: "When I first saw that the people of my town were not listening to me, I examined my ways. Next I realized that my own family was not listening to me. I examined my ways further, and found that I was to blame, because I was not acting properly. I then worked hard at improving myself. When my family members saw this, they began listening to me, and eventually the people of my town began to listen to me as well."

⋙ Why They Follow Him

Two prominent rebbes once met at a resort in Eastern Europe. As they began talking, one complained that he had very few followers. The other one, however, had a very large following.

"I understand," said the first, "that people believe you capable of all types of wondrous actions: healing the sick, aiding those in distress, and even reading people's minds. I wonder if you can really do any of these. Can you, for example, tell me what I am thinking of right now?"

"Of course," said the second. "You're reflecting on the verse in *Tehillim*, 'I have placed Hashem before me always.' "

"You're wrong," said the first rebbe. "That's not I was thinking about."

"That," stated the second, "explains why you don't have people flocking to you."

⋙ Teaching Torah for Free

R' David Kronglas, the *Mashgiach* of Ner Israel, used to say, "If I were to acquire a large amount of money, it wouldn't change my life in the slightest. I'd use it to repay the yeshiva for the salary I have received over the years."

◄§ Pure Logic

R' Levi Yitzchak of Berdichev used to say, "If the *halachah* states clearly that one must always give every individual the benefit of the doubt, how much more is it true that one must always give the community the benefit of the doubt."

Rabbinic Judgments

◄§ A Greater Loss

Whenever a *kashrus* question was brought to R' Feitel, the Slonim *dayan*, he would consult with R' Eizel Charif, the *rav* of the town. Once, a difficult question arose concerning an ox that had been slaughtered. R' Feitel and R' Eizel discussed the question at length. R' Feitel leaned towards the lenient view, and felt that the meat could be eaten, while R' Eizel insisted that the meat was not kosher. "But the principle of *hefsed merubah* (major financial loss) should tip the scales here," argued R' Feitel.

R' Eizel answered: "When one rules that non-kosher meat is kosher, the loss is far greater."

⋑ A Test

Soon after R' Chaim Halberstam became the *rav* of Sanz, he was asked to summon R' Yudel, the richest man in town, to a *din Torah*. R' Chaim immediately sent his *shamash* to ask R' Yudel to appear before him. R' Yudl told the *shamash* he had no time and sent the *shamash* away.

R' Chaim sent the *shamash* back to tell R' Yudel to appear immediately. This time R' Yudel screamed at the *shamash*, "Tell the *rav* I'm busy! I can't come now!"

Finally, R' Chaim sent the *shamash* with an ultimatum to R' Yudel: Either come immediately or you will be put in *cherem* — excommunicated.

R' Yudel rushed over to R' Chaim. When he arrived, he and the man who had summoned him to the *din Torah* told R' Chaim that the entire "case" was a put-up job.

"Rebbe," said R' Yudel, "I simply wanted to be sure that we have a *rav* who will stand up for what is right, even if it means taking on the mighty and the wealthy of the town."

⋑ An Obedient Community

The leaders of the Jewish community in Jerusalem came to R' Shmuel Salant, the *rav* of the city, and complained that there were people who went for walks on Shabbos outside the walls of the city (in those days, most Jews lived within the city walls). Some of them were even carrying things with them in contravention of the *halachah*. The leaders urged R' Shmuel to forbid walks outside the city walls to prevent problems of carrying on Shabbos.

R' Shmuel rejected their request out of hand. "I'm afraid for those who might go for walks even though I've forbidden it," he said. "As long as we haven't made an issue of it and brought it to their attention, what they're doing is *shogeg* — an unintentional sin. But if I forbid people from going for walks, those who disobey me will be sinning with the full knowledge of what they're doing.

"But rabbi," the communal leaders continued, "why do you think people would deliberately disobey you? Every edict you've issued has been obeyed by everyone."

"The reason for that," said R' Shmuel, "is that I've never issued an edict that I thought might be disobeyed."

◄§ On the Other Hand

The *Chasam Sofer* used to say: "A leader who wishes to be obeyed must ensure that 'his voice is heard' (*Shemos* 28:35). There are times when he has to be willing to raise his voice and tell people what they should do, without being intimidated. Otherwise, people will not respect him."

◄§ I'm Willing to Accept Such Complaints

R' Avraham Abush of Frankfurt was known for his efforts to find a lenient path in cases of great financial loss. Prior to one of the festivals, a question was brought to his *beis din* regarding the slaughtered animal of a very poor man. The other members of the *beis din* ruled that the animal was *treif* on the basis of a clear ruling by the *Rama*. But R' Avraham Abush kept searching for a way to permit the eating of the animal.

Finally, R' Avraham Abush found a way to permit the use of the animal, but could not persuade his fellow judges, who felt that the *Rama's* ruling was the controlling precedent. "The *Rama's* ruling doesn't concern me," R' Avraham Abush declared. "In the next world, when the *Rama* complains that I ruled against his view, I'm sure I'll find a way to appease him. What I'm afraid of is coming to the next world and having the poor man, who owned the animal, complaining against me for having caused him such a large loss."

◄§ "Modern-Day Rulings"

Traditionally, Poland did not have any large yeshivos. Instead a number of men studied Torah all day and night in each *shul* and *beis medrash*. Thus, when R' Meir Shapiro founded Yeshivas Chachmei Lublin, he encountered much opposition.

He was once asked why he had undertaken such a dramatic departure from the prevailing custom. He replied, "I was afraid that if I didn't establish a yeshiva in Poland, Torah learning would decline so much that the rabbis would not know how to rule on a chicken brought to them and would resort to soothsaying instead. They would open a *Chumash* at random, and if the first letter was a *kuf*, they would rule the chicken is kosher, and if the first letter was a *tet*, they would rule it *treif*."

⋅§ *Preparation*

Whenever R' Moshe Feinstein had to rule on a question which dealt with *pikuach nefesh* — danger to human life — he fasted the entire day before ruling.

⋅§ *A Wagon Driver Remains a Wagon Driver*

Two men came to the *Noda B'Yehudah* for a *din Torah*. The first to speak was dressed as a simple wagon driver. He began, "Rabbi, I hired this man to drive me to Prague. Along the way, as we were traveling through a dense forest, he pounced on me, stole everything I had, and forced me to change clothes with him."

The man dressed as a wealthy merchant replied, "The man is insane and suffers from delusions. For the past two days, he has been running after me throughout the city, and I can't figure out how to get rid of him."

The *Noda B'Yehudah* examined each man separately, but was unable to discern who was telling the truth. Finally, he told them to return the next morning.

The next morning, immediately after their prayers, the two came to the *Rav*'s study. The *shamash* had them sit outside on a bench and wait. Half an hour passed, an hour, two hours, and they still were not summoned. Inside the office, they heard the *Noda B'Yehudah* learning and pacing back and forth. It was as if he had forgotten about them. After many hours waiting in this fashion, the *Noda B'Yehudah* suddenly flung open the door and exclaimed, "Wagon driver, come here!" The man in the elegant clothes stood up without thinking, and the problem was solved.

⊷§ *Deserving of Punishment*

R' Yaakov of Lissa once stayed over in a certain inn. Outside the wind was raging, so he curled up close to the fire. As he lay there, he saw the local *shochet* enter. The man had been summoned by the innkeeper to slaughter a calf, but decided to first warm up. He took a glass of wine. That did not do the trick, so he took another — and then another and another.

When the *shochet* finally arose to slaughter the calf, R' Yaakov advised him to first take a short nap since it is forbidden to *shecht* when one is drunk.

Not realizing who R' Yaakov was, the *shochet* told him to mind his own business.

R' Yaakov replied, "I owe you a debt of gratitude. You've cleared up a long-standing question. In the *Haggadah*, in *Chad Gadya*, I can understand why the cat and the dog and the stick and the rest were all punished. But why was the *shochet* punished for slaughtering the cow? After all, when a *shochet* slaughters an animal, he even recites a blessing before doing so.

"Now I finally can understand why the *shochet* was punished — for slaughtering an animal after partaking of the four cups of wine."

⊷§ *Life Preservers*

A construction worker in *Eretz Yisrael* once asked R' Shlomo of Baranovich whether he was required to wear *tzitzis* in the blazing heat when drenched in sweat. "*Chazal* teach," said R' Shlomo, "that a person who wears *tefillin* and *tzitzis*, and who has a *mezuzah* on his door, 'will not easily sin.' Imagine yourself in the ocean, being tossed about by powerful waves. Would you throw off your life preserver?"

◄§ The Wrong Address

Chassidim of the Vizhnitzer Rebbe asked him to recommend a *rav* for their town. The Rebbe immediately gave them the name of one of his students, a brilliant young *talmid chacham*. A few days later, the chassidim returned. "Rebbe," they said, "we asked him to come for an interview, and we saw that he is little more than a boy — and a very frail one at that. Could you suggest someone else?"

"Now that I know your requirements," said the Rebbe, "I have the perfect candidate for you. Here is his name and address." The second man turned out to be the local butcher, a middle-aged man who was as strong as an ox but completely unlearned.

◄§ What the Master's Son Wants

A man on his deathbed was afraid that his slave would not hand over the estate to his son, but would steal it for himself. He then wrote a will which stated that his entire estate would belong to the slave — with the son permitted to take only one item of the estate for himself.

After the father's death, when the son found out about the provisions of the will, he became very upset and ran to the *rav* for advice. "Rabbi," he said, "my father left his entire fortune to his slave. All I am allowed to have is one item. What should I do?"

"My son," said the *rav*, "your father was a very wise man. By writing his will the way he did, he made sure that the slave would not squander all your money in your absence. As to which item to select as your own, I suggest you select the slave, for the law is that whatever is owned by a slave belongs to his master."

✺ You Have to See Both Sides

The Jews of the Old Yishuv in *Eretz Yisrael* lived off the *chalukah* — funds donated by Jews throughout the world to enable them to remain in *Eretz Yisrael* and learn Torah.

Once, a number of students brought a man to R' Shmuel Salanter. The man's face was bloody and he had obviously been punched quite a few times. "Rabbi," the students said, "this man was beaten by so-and-so. Look at how badly he was hurt. Don't you think the other man's *chalukah* funding should be suspended until he is tried for beating this man?"

"That's all very well," replied R' Shmuel, "but what about the other man? For all we know, he didn't come to complain because he was beaten so badly by this man that he was simply unable to walk."

R' Shmuel then sent his *shamash* to the other man's home, and the *shamash* soon reported back that the other man had been beaten even more brutally. "My children," R' Shmuel told his sheepish students, "let this be a lesson for you. Never judge a case until you've heard both sides."

✺ The Proper Frame of Mind

The *Maharshal*, R' Shlomo Luria, whose comments are found in the back of the Vilna Talmud and who was one of the greatest scholars of his time, had a unique way of preparing to judge *dinei Torah* that came before him. Before the *din Torah* began, he would always go to a certain *rav*, who would admonish him for all his sins. The *Maharshal* would sit with his head bowed, listening attentively to every word. Only after the *rav* was done would the *Maharshal* enter to judge the case.

✑ When to Delay the Answer

If someone asked R' David Kronglas whether it was permissible to do something and R' David thought it was forbidden, he always answered, "I have to study this further. I'll get back to you." He explained that it was too difficult for him to tell a person something was categorically forbidden. He would check out the sources another time, and only afterward call the person back and tell him that the matter was forbidden. On the other hand, if something was permitted, he would immediately tell the person the *halachah*.

✑ A Serious Question

R' Shmuel Salanter was once lecturing in his yeshiva when a woman came to him with a question. "Rebbe," she said, "I left some meat which had not been *kashered* on a ledge and my cat stole it. What is the status of the cat?"

The students of the yeshiva could barely contain their mirth at this ridiculous question. But R' Shmuel treated her query like any other. He took out a volume of the *Shulchan Aruch*, studied it pensively for a while, and told the woman, "The cat is *treif*. From now on you should be more careful not to leave meat unattended."

After the woman had left, R' Shmuel told his students, "You will have to rule one day on a wide variety of questions. You must treat each question, no matter how silly, with the utmost seriousness. If you laugh at someone's question, he or she will never again consult you, even when there is a serious halachic question."

✑ Not Even for a Sultan

R' Chaim ben Attar was once hearing a case between two very high-ranking Jews in his native Morocco. In the midst of the trial, one of the disputants left the courtroom and came back some time later with no less a personage than the sultan himself. Seeing the sultan, R' Chaim told the other judges, "You are to continue with the case as if nothing had happened."

After the case had ended, R' Chaim turned to the sultan and said to him, "Welcome, your majesty."

Upon hearing this, the sultan became very annoyed. "If you didn't know who I was, I can understand your not having interrupted the case to welcome me," he said, "but as you obviously did know who I am, why did you just go on with the case?"

"Your majesty," replied R' Chaim, "We are commanded by the King of kings that 'you shall not recognize anyone in judgment,' and as long as our case was in session I could not even acknowledge your presence. Now that it is over, I am delighted to welcome you to our midst."

⋙ The First Time I Have Ever Seen You

When R' Shmelke of Nikolsburg judged a case, he always kept his *tallis* over his head and eyes.

He once met a famous *talmid chacham*, who was sure R' Shmelke would recognize him as he had recently been involved before him in a legal case. R' Shmelke, though, told him, "I never see the face of any litigant who comes before me in judgment. This is the first time I have ever seen you."

⋙ It's a Riddle

R' Eizel Charif, who was often quite cutting in his remarks to the wealthy and to the heads of the community, nevertheless showed a great deal of sympathy to the poor.

Once, in a court case between a rich man and a poor man, R' Eizel ruled in favor of the poor man. The rich man, furious at having lost, berated R' Eizel and said, "I don't understand why you always stick up for the poor."

"Actually," said R' Eizel, "I've been bothered by a similar question for a long time! Why is it that most times the law is in favor of the poor man?"

Assimilationists and Reformers

✌ Who Is Modern?

R' Yitzchak Elchanan Spektor once had to take a train trip. On that same train was a "modern Jew," one who had "modernized" his Judaism by throwing away most of it.

As the train entered the Vilna station, the "modern" man saw that the entire train platform, as far as the eye could see, was packed with people. "Surely there must be some member of the royalty on the train," he thought, "or maybe a high government dignitary." When he asked who everyone had come to see, though, he was told that all were waiting to catch a glimpse of R' Yitzchak Elchanan.

"Well, if he's on the train, I can understand it," thought the man to himself. "He's one of our leading rabbis, and I've read of how he meets with the greatest of dignitaries."

Determined to see this great rabbi for himself, the man went over to the first-class carriage. How could so distinguished a rabbi travel in anything less?

"No, there's no one here by that name," replied the conductor.

"Well, maybe he's in the second-class carriage," thought the man. "I'll look for him there." Again he was unsuccessful.

Finally, the man went to the third-class carriage. "Yes, he's here," a man told him, pointing to an old Jew with a long white beard standing in the corner. And what an embarrassment! He was standing there *davening,* in his *tallis* and *tefillin* — right in front of all the non-Jews!

The man waited until R' Yitzchak Elchanan had ended his prayers and then went over and introduced himself.

"Rabbi," he said, "I'd heard so much about you and what you've done for the Jewish people that I had always thought of you as someone who is modern."

"Indeed I am," said R' Yitzchak Elchanan. "Those people who keep the *mitzvos* are the modern ones. It is the Jews who don't keep the *mitzvos* who are old fashioned, having reverted back to the practices of Avraham's father Terach, who was an idol worshiper."

⪧ A Sieve Without Holes

A group of *maskilim* attempted to provoke the Dubno *Maggid* by asking him to teach them *Shir HaShirim* — the Song of Songs — "without any allegories."

"Let me tell you a story," responded the *Maggid*. "A newly married young man was sent by his father-in-law to the local fair, with orders to buy a certain quantity of fabrics. Time and time again his father-in-law stressed, 'You must take each bolt and examine it carefully. If you find any holes in it, don't buy it.'

"His mother-in-law, too, gave him a list of things to buy for the kitchen, among them a sieve. When the son-in-law came back, he brought back everything that had been ordered — except the sieve. His mother-in-law asked him why he had forgotten the sieve. 'I checked many sieves. Every single one of them had holes, and I was warned to check for holes,' the young man explained.

" 'Fool,' said the mother-in-law, 'a sieve requires holes. If it doesn't have holes, it's not a sieve.'

"By the same token," said the *Maggid*, "all of *Shir HaShirim* is one long allegory. If you to try to study it without the allegorical meaning, it's not *Shir HaShirim*. It's a sieve without holes."

◄§ Avraham's Clothes

A man who mocked the chassidim once asked R' Simchah Bunim of Pshischa: "Rebbe, what type of clothes did our forefather Avraham wear? Do you think he wore a *kapote* and a *shtreimel*?"

"I'm not sure what Avraham wore," said R' Simchah Bunim, "but I do know how he chose his clothes. He looked at what the non-Jews around him were wearing, and picked a garb which was completely different from theirs."

◄§ Copying the Goyim

R' Yonasan Eybeschuetz once met a Jew who had abandoned his people's ways to such an extent that he refused to have his son circumcised. When R' Yonasan asked him to explain his refusal, he answered, "Circumcision is not even a Jewish law. Modern scholars have shown that the Egyptians had their sons circumcised. When the Jews were in Egypt, they learned this custom from the Egyptians. Why do I have to keep an Egyptian custom?"

"Well, to a certain extent I agree with you," said R' Yonasan. "Indeed, the Egyptians did have their sons circumcised. My source, though, is not your 'modern-day scholars,' but no less an authority than *Rashi*, who states clearly that Yosef ordered the Egyptians to circumcise their sons."

"That makes no sense," said the man. "What possible reason would Yosef have had to make the Egyptians circumcise their sons?"

"On the contrary," said R' Yonasan, "Yosef did so because of his great brilliance. He saw that a time would come when the freethinkers would abandon all Jewish observance and slavishly imitate every non-Jewish custom. By requiring circumcision among the Egyptians, he hoped that the freethinkers would at least retain circumcision as a respectable Egyptian custom!"

⋅§ *Do You Want Good Grammar?*

A *maskil* once complained to the *Chafetz Chaim* that in the *chadarim* children were not taught Hebrew grammar. He argued that the *chadarim* should study less Talmud and spend more time on Hebrew grammar. "After all, Rebbe," he said, "*Chazal* tell us that if a person pronounces the *Shema* correctly, his punishment in *Gehinnom* is reduced."

"What you are quoting from *Chazal*," said the *Chafetz Chaim*, "is not their only statement concerning *Shema*. If a person reads the *Shema* without perfect grammatic exactitude, he has still fulfilled his obligation, although it is not ideal. On the other hand, if a person knows perfect grammar but doesn't recite *Shema* [an obvious reference to the *maskilim*, many of whom had thrown off all the *mitzvos*], he has not fulfilled his obligation. You should remind your friends who violate so many other Torah laws that even if they read the *Shema* perfectly, a reduced punishment in *Gehinnom* is still *Gehinnom*."

◄§ Elementary Knowledge

A *maskil* once came to R' Eizel Charif and complained that the *chadarim* refused to study secular subjects, such as arithmetic, that are needed in everyday life.

"That's not true," replied R' Eizel, "these children know more arithmetic than you do." The *maskil* challenged R' Eizel to prove his claim. "Very simple," said R' Eizel, "I can ask every child in *cheder* what day of the *Omer* it is today and receive the correct answer, but can you tell me?"

◄§ "Enjoy, Enjoy!"

The *Chiddushei HaRim* and the *rav* of Warsaw, R' Dov Ber Meisels, once came to a wealthy man seeking a contribution to an important cause. Seeing him eating lunch, they told him, "Enjoy, enjoy!"

"Rabbis," the man answered, "I doubt you would wish me to enjoy my food if you knew that it isn't kosher."

"On the contrary," replied the *Chiddushei HaRim*, "since the food is not kosher, I really hope you enjoy it. If not, that would mean you were eating it to show your contempt for *mitzvos,* and that is a far worse sin."

◄§ Esav's Blessing

"Why is it," a *maskil* asked R' Shalom of Belz, "that those Jews who have discarded our traditional garb and wear modern clothes do much better financially than those who don't?"

"Simple," R' Shalom answered. "When Yaakov received the blessing of Esav, he discarded his traditional clothes and put on Esav's clothes."

ᴥ Half the Truth

A *maskil* complained to the *Netziv* that even though *Chazal* tell us that "one who speaks the holy tongue is guaranteed a portion in the World-to-Come," all the religious Jews shunned the various societies which had sprung up to encourage the use of Hebrew as an everyday tongue.

"You're absolutely right," said the *Netziv*, "but for some reason you neglected to quote the second half of the *Chazal*, 'One who recites the *Shema* in the morning and evening is guaranteed a place in the World-to-Come.' "

ᴥ He Really Means It

The *Malbim* noticed that one of the freethinkers in the community always recited the blessing on receiving an *aliyah* to the Torah with great devotion, laying special stress on the passage, "Who has chosen us from all the nations and given us His Torah."

"The reason for his love of these words is simple," said the *Malbim*. "He thanks Hashem that He gave us the Torah, so that he feels free to totally ignore it. Had Hashem given the gentiles the Torah, he would feel obligated to observe its laws."

ᴥ In a Land Which Is Not Theirs

R' Menachem Mendel of Kotzk was very much opposed to the emancipation of the Jews throughout Europe in the wake of Napoleon's armies. He explained the verse, *Your seed will be strangers in a land which is not theirs,* as follows: "As long as they are in a land 'not their own' they will remain 'your seed.' "

ᴥ It Depends Upon When It Was Given

R' Zvi Hirsh Charif was once talking to David Friedlander, an early Reformer. At the time, the Reformers had not yet set up separate places of worship, and they were trying to introduce various changes in the traditional synagogues — all "in the spirit of the times." Friedlander told R' Zvi Hirsh, "Rabbi, I am sure that had Moshe Rabbeinu lived in our times, he would have agreed to the changes we want to introduce."

"Let me tell you a story," said R' Zvi Hirsh. "Once a merchant wished to travel to a very important fair. He hired a local coachman to take him there with all his goods. However, the merchant made one stipulation: If the coachman did not get him to the fair on time, not only would he not be paid, but he would have to pay the merchant for the loss of income involved.

"Unfortunately, there was a tremendous snowstorm, and the coachman was unable to get the merchant to the fair on time. The merchant thereupon sued the coachman for his losses. When the case came before the local *beis din*, the *beis din* ruled according to the merchant. The coachman, however, was not reconciled to the *beis din*'s ruling, and turned to the *rav* with a question. 'Rabbi,' he asked, 'what date was the Torah given?' 'The sixth of *Sivan*,' the *rav* told him. 'That explains everything,' said the coachman. 'The sixth of *Sivan* is in the middle of the summer. Had the Torah been given in the winter, your ruling would have been in accordance with me.'

"And you," R' Zvi Hirsh finished, "are acting like that coachman."

◈§ *It's Cold!*

R' Avraham of Sochachov once visited the health spa in Neuheim. On Shabbos morning, he took a stroll, wearing his Shabbos *shtreimel*. On his walk, he met the Reform "rabbi" of the town, a man who could not bear the dress of traditional Jews.

"Why are you wearing a hot fur hat on such a warm summer day?" asked the Reformer.

"Because Shabbos is so cold in this city," replied R' Avraham.

↝ Keeping the Pigs Out

A freethinker once asked R' Chaim, "Why do religious Jews insist on wearing beards? That is such an old-fashioned custom. Doesn't a shaven chin look much nicer and tidier?"

R' Chaim answered, "When you walk out into the countryside, why do you find fences around the different fields? After all, wouldn't fields without fences look far more attractive? The answer, obviously, is that fences are put up to keep the pigs out. And that is the same reason we wear beards!"

↝ Men of Truth

The leaders of the Jewish community in Brisk came to R' Yosef Ber and complained that heresy was spreading rapidly in the town. "I'm not surprised," said R' Yosef Ber, "truth always has a way of winning."

"What do you mean, 'truth?' " they asked incredulously. "Do you consider heresy to be truth?"

"Not at all," said R' Yosef Ber, "but the heretics *truly* believe their heresy, and fight with all their might for others to accept their views. Among those who observe the *mitzvos*, on the other hand, not all *truly* believe in what they profess, and their efforts are therefore halfhearted. Unfortunately, we have many people fighting for the real truth in a *false* way, and that is why the other side manages to score its successes."

↝ Missing the Boat

A *maskil* once asked R' Eizel of Slonim, "Rav, why is it that the freethinkers are much better-mannered than those who are learned in Torah?"

"The reason is simple," said R' Eizel. "When the Jews were about to receive the Torah, they were told by Moshe, 'Be ready!' Most of the Jews immediately dropped what they were doing and hurried over to receive the Torah. They stood there from the beginning to the end. Of course, there was a vast amount to absorb, and occasionally they did not place enough emphasis on certain parts of the Torah.

"On the other hand, when the *maskilim* of those days heard the command, 'Be ready,' they went to their tents, changed into their best clothes, washed up and combed their hair, and then strolled leisurely over to where the Torah was being given. By the time they arrived, the giving of the Torah was nearly complete, and all they heard was the small tractate of *Derech Eretz* — proper manners. Ever since, they have concentrated on that and that alone."

⊷§ Only as Much as They Can Bear

R' Chaim Hirsh Mannheimer was the *rav* of Ungvar. There were two *shuls* in town — a traditional one, where many chassidim *davened*, and a "modern" synagogue. As was the custom, R' Chaim Hirsh gave *derashos* on the Shabbos before Pesach and the Shabbos before Yom Kippur. However, as there were two *shuls* in town, R' Chaim Hirsh spoke twice each day, in the morning at the more "modern" *shul*, and in the afternoon at the traditional one.

It soon became known that his message varied between the two *shuls*. His tone in the more "modern" *shul* was moderate, while in the traditional *shul* his tone was stern, and he demanded much more of the people. When he was asked why he reserved his more severe admonitions for the traditional *shul*, rather than for the members of the "modern" *shul*, who were more lax in their observances of the *mitzvos*, he explained:

"A wagon driver once told me that he had two horses hitched to his wagon, one a hard-working, fleet horse and the other a lazy, slow horse. Whenever he came to a steep hill, he whipped the fast horse, and they were soon over the hill. On one occasion, the wagon driver was lost in thought. The wagon reached a particularly steep hill, and he began whipping the wrong horse. The lazy horse came to a full stop, reared up its hind legs, and almost kicked him in the face. By a miracle, he didn't lose an eye or a few teeth.

"I don't think I need to go on and draw the parallel," said R' Chaim Hirsh.

◆§ Partners With Amalek

With a few notable exceptions, the Jews of Berlin were not known for their observance of *halachah*. In fact, a number of the "kosher" butchers had been caught selling non-kosher meat in their stores. To justify their actions, the butchers claimed that they would suffer heavy losses if they had to sell a large animal that had been found to be *treif* to a non-Jewish butcher. Since the non-Jewish butchers knew they were unable to use the animal themselves, they would pay only a fraction of its true value.

When R' Zvi Hirsh Charif of Halberstadt served as the *rav* of Berlin, he thought of a way to solve the problem. He gathered together a number of Jewish and non-Jewish butchers, and suggested a business deal: the non-Jewish butchers would became partners with the Jewish butchers in the sale of kosher meat so that they would make a profit on the kosher meat as well. In return, they would pledge to buy at the going price, any animal found to be *treif*.

After much bargaining, a deal was struck along these lines. R' Zvi Hirsh then issued a certificate of *kashrus* to the kosher butchers, which read: "Kosher meat, in partnership with Amalek."

When the butchers read what R' Zvi Hirsh had written, they were furious. "Rabbi," they said, "are you trying to make fun of us? What do you mean by 'in partnership with Amalek?' "

"On the contrary," said R' Zvi Hirsh, "I meant it to reflect well on you. I am telling everyone that you can be trusted because you are 'in partnership with Amalek,' and therefore there is no temptation on your part to try to sell non-kosher meat as kosher."

~§ Paying up an IOU

The early Reformers in Germany came to R' Azriel Hildesheimer and appealed to him to agree to the changes they wanted to make in the prayer service. After all, they argued, the services were too long and burdensome. If the services were shortened, people would be more ready to come to the synagogue to pray.

"Let me tell you a story," said R' Hildesheimer. "A man owed a considerable amount of money to another. Realizing that he was bankrupt and would never be able to repay the money, he appealed to his creditor to reduce the amount he owed. Eventually, after much negotiation, the creditor agreed to accept, on a specified day, half the amount owed him.

"Came the appointed day, and rather than paying, the debtor offered the creditor an IOU for half the original amount. 'I'm not willing to accept that,' said the creditor. 'If you pay cash, I'll willing to settle for half the amount. However, if you wish to give me an IOU, it will have to be for the full amount.'

"And the same is true here. I know that even if we settled for a shortened synagogue service, your people would still not come to pray on a regular basis. That being the case, let the service remain the way it has always been."

~§ Rasha!

The *Chiddushei HaRim* was told that a certain young man, who had been a brilliant scholar, had joined the *maskilim* and thrown off the yoke of the Torah. Nevertheless, he ordered his chassidim not to say anything disparaging about the young man until he himself had a chance to meet with him.

Some time later, the *Chiddushei HaRim* went to visit the young man. The two remained locked together for hours, until the *Chiddushei HaRim* emerged and called out, "*Rasha*! — wicked one!"

The *Chiddushei HaRim* explained later to his chassidim why he had acted as he had. "I learned this from Moshe at Sinai," he said. "When Hashem told Moshe that his people had become corrupted, Moshe did not condemn them. Instead, he waited until he came close to the camp. Only when he actually saw the people dancing around the Golden Calf did Moshe become angry and throw down the Tablets. Why? Because as long as he was far away, he felt that once the people saw him, they might repent. However, when he came into view and they still did not repent, he threw down the Tablets.

"Here too," he concluded, "I thought that if the young man met with me, his Rebbe, face to face, he might yet repent. When I saw that even that made no difference, I knew there was no hope, and I let all know that he is indeed a *rasha*."

⤳ Still Not Kosher

Daniel Chwolson, a Russian Jew, converted to Christianity in order to further his career. He later became a professor of Oriental languages in St. Petersburg. Once his reputation was firmly established, he devoted much of his life to defending the Jews against various charges, such as the blood libels. He even spent time in Torah study.

The *Netziv* was asked his opinion of this very unusual *meshumad* (convert from Judaism).

"It's very hard for me to say exactly," said the *Netziv*, "and I'll tell you a story to explain myself.

"Once, a very pious Jew became ill. The doctors who examined him decided that there was only one way to cure him: He had to eat pork. 'Never,' said the man, and his pious wife echoed him.

"But his health deteriorated even further, and he became critically ill. Again the doctors were called, and again the same verdict: He had to eat pork. The *rav* was called in and agreed — in these circumstances, not only could he eat pork, but he *had* to, for saving a human life takes precedence.

"The wife, too, finally agreed, but she made a condition: The *rav* had to arrange for the local *shochet* to slaughter a pig, 'according to *halachah*.'

"The *shochet* slaughtered the animal 'according to *halachah*,' but now the wife insisted that the pig's lungs be checked, the same way the lungs of cattle are checked to ensure that they are not *treif*.

"The *shochet* complied, but when he examined the lungs, he found something suspicious. He couldn't decide how to rule, and called the *rav* to examine the lungs.

"The *rav* looked and looked, turned the lungs this way and that, but said nothing. Finally, the *shochet* said, '*Nu,* rabbi?' 'I have a problem,' said the *rav.* 'If these had been the lungs of a cow, I would have pronounced it kosher, but how can I say that about a pig? As 'kosher' as the lungs may appear, they're still the lungs of a pig and it is still *treif*.'

"And that," said the *Netziv*, "is my attitude to Chwolson."

✤ *Selling Out*

Professor Chwolson was an apostate who nevertheless maintained contacts with many prominent Jews, including rabbis, and devoted much time to helping Jews in distress. He signed his letters to his Jewish friends, "Yosef," his name before his conversion.

When he celebrated his fiftieth birthday, greetings streamed in from throughout Russia to mark this event. Many Jewish communities joined in the congratulations. None, however, were forthcoming from Brisk. R' Chaim Soloveitchik, the *rav* of the town, refused to allow any congratulatory message to be sent.

When Chwolson realized that he had been snubbed, he sent a short, one-line sentence to R' Chaim, quoting a verse, "Yosef recognized his brothers, but they did not recognize him."

R' Chaim sent back a short reply: "There's a major difference. In the Torah, the brothers sold out Yosef. In this case, Yosef sold out his brothers."

⊷ Something to Envy

R' Azriel Hildesheimer used to say: "There are three things about the freethinkers that I envy. They are never guilty of mentioning Hashem's name in vain, they never find themselves in doubt about whether to recite a blessing or not, and they can think Torah thoughts in a place where one is forbidden to do so."

⊷ Somewhat Like Noah's Ark

R' Samson Raphael Hirsch once had to spend some time in a certain health resort. It so happened that the only synagogue was a lavish building erected by the Reformers. R' Hirsch, of course, would not pray in a Reform temple. He told the spiritual leader of the temple that his health made it impossible to pray inside the building. Instead, he would pray in the park outside the temple.

Later, after the prayer service, the spiritual leader of the temple, very proud of the new building, asked R' Hirsch what he thought of the temple.

"Well," said R' Hirsch, "in some ways it resembles Noah's ark and in some ways it doesn't. It resembles the ark in that it has *kofer* (literally pitch — but here used to imply *kefirah*, heresy) both inside and outside. On the other hand, it doesn't resemble Noah's ark, because the ark was used to save the world, and I doubt if this building will even save the Judaism of the present generation, not to speak of the next generation."

⊷ Strange Coexistence

R' Yaakov Ettlinger was told about a certain Jew who ate *treif* food, and yet was known far and wide as a donor to every worthy charity. R' Yaakov pondered for a few moments and said, "I find it astounding that a kosher heart and a *treif* stomach can coexist in the same body."

ᴥᔑ Strong Medicine

A *maskil* approached R' Yosef Ber of Brisk and asked him why the rabbis had the right to add all types of restrictions which are not specified in the Torah. After all, he said, the Torah states clearly, "You may not add."

"First of all," said R' Yosef Ber, "we deduce from the words, 'You shall observe my charge,' that we are allowed to add a charge to the Torah charge — i.e., to add *gezeiros* (regulations) to the Torah law — and, in fact, the Torah immediately thereafter specifies that by doing so, 'You will not be committing a sin.'

"Furthermore, the Torah is a medicine to us — the medicine that keeps us alive. If a person takes more of the medicine than the doctor tells him to — sometimes even a drop too much — that can be harmful to him. On the other hand, once the patient has taken the medicine, he is allowed to drink as much tea as he wishes, without it affecting him. The Torah law is like medicine, and we may not add even a drop to it. On the other hand, all the extra rules and regulations of the rabbis are like the tea one drinks after taking the medicine of the Torah law."

ᴥᔑ We Know Exactly What They Mean

The Czarist Russian government did everything it could to force the Jews to abandon their religion and convert, but failed miserably in its efforts. Finally, it decided to use the *maskilim* to bring the message of "modernism" to the Jews in the towns and villages throughout Russia. Teams of *maskilim* were sent all over with a simple message: All the *chadarim* should devote much of their time to secular studies, while the yeshivos should be converted into factories, their students supplying the labor force. This way, the yeshivah students could be "gainfully employed." Everywhere they went, the *maskilim* were met with scorn and contempt. In many towns, they were not permitted to speak at all.

One such group of *maskilim* came to Volozhin, and were surprised to find that the *Netziv* was actually ready to meet with them. When they met, the leader of the delegation complained about the way they were being treated in the different communities, especially when they had come with a message of such importance and of such great benefit to the Jewish people. After all, they claimed, such a revolution in Jewish education might even lead the government to grant the Jews emancipation one day.

When the leader of the *maskilim* finished speaking, the *Netziv* told him simply, "Even if by some chance there might be any small theoretical benefit to be gained by doing what you suggest, we have to remember only one thing — the source of this 'marvelous plan.' It comes from the Russian government, and that government has never yet been known to do anything that might in any way help the Jews. Thus, I have no doubt that the plan was not meant to help us, but to help the Russian government in its attempt to have all the Jews ultimately convert."

↜§ What Do We Have in Common?

R' Moshe Yitzchak, the *Maggid* of Kelm, once came to a seaside resort where the Jews were very lax in their Torah observance. Called upon to speak in the local synagogue, R' Moshe Yitzchak gave a fiery speech in which he pleaded with the people to repent their sins. The next day, the head of the community, who was clean-shaven — at that time a sure sign of Reformist tendencies — came to the inn where R' Moshe Yitzchak was staying. "Rabbi," the man said, "when you speak, you should be more moderate in tone. You're scaring the people." R' Moshe Yitzchak listened to the man and said, "I'd like to tell you a story."

"I was once walking along the road, when I came across a bull. The bull stretched out its hoof and wished to shake my hand. 'Bull,' I said, 'why should I shake your hoof? What do we have in common?' 'You eat my meat,' replied the bull. 'You are correct,' I said, so I shook its hoof and went on. Soon I came across a cow. The cow, too, extended its hoof in greeting. 'Cow,' I said, 'why should I shake your hoof? What do we have in common?' 'You drink my milk,' replied the cow. 'You are correct,' I said, so I shook its hoof and went on. Soon I came across a goat. The goat stretched out its hoof and wished to shake my hand. 'Goat,' I said, 'why should I shake your hoof? What do we have in common?' 'You and I both have beards,' replied the goat. 'You are correct,' I said, so I shook its hoof and went on. Soon I came across a pig. The pig, too, extended its hoof in greeting. I became very angry. 'Pig,' I said, 'why should I shake your hoof? I don't eat your meat or drink your milk, nor do you have a beard. What do we have in common?' "

☙ "We'd Be in Tatters"

R' Yechiel Michel of Gustinin came to visit his rebbe, the *Chiddushei HaRim*, in Warsaw. When he arrived in the city, he immediately went to the inn where he would be staying. As he entered the inn, he saw a group of freethinkers playing cards and making fun of all the greatest rebbes, including his own.

Terribly upset, R' Yechiel Michel rushed out of the inn, but now he had a real question: Was he obligated to tear *kriyah* on his clothes after what he had heard? On the other hand, was it proper to appear before the *Chiddushei HaRim* with his clothes torn?

Not knowing what to do, R' Yechiel Michel went over to the *beis midrash* and sought an answer to his dilemma in the halachic codes. As much as he searched, however, he could not find a definitive ruling.

Finally, R' Yechiel Michel went over to the *Chiddushei HaRim* and asked him what he had to do.

"Yechiel Michel," said the *Chiddushei HaRim*, "if we had to tear *kriyah* every time some freethinker insulted us, we'd be walking around in tattered clothing our whole lives."

◆§ What's in a Name?

A chassid came to R' Zvi Hirsh of Liska for a blessing for his children. "And what are their names?" asked the rebbe.

"Ignacz, Stephen, and Julius," replied the chassid.

"Why don't you call them by their Jewish names?" the rebbe asked him.

"Rebbe," the chassid replied, "can't a person be a perfectly good Jew and observe all the *mitzvos* even if he doesn't have a Hebrew name?"

"Let me explain myself to you," said R' Hirshele. "I am named after my forefathers, and have a fine Jewish name. Yet I find it hard to fulfill all the *mitzvos* properly. Imagine how much harder it must be for a person who uses a non-Jewish name, a name often taken from the saints of other religions or from pagan sources."

◆§ From Whom Will They Learn?

One of the Jewish storekeepers in Ostraha kept his store open on Shabbos. The Rebbe summoned the man to try to persuade him to change his ways. This man, however, had been thoroughly infected by the winds of "modernism" and refused to yield. In fact, he had the *chutzpah* to answer the Rebbe: "You too are a sinner. I know that you fast a number of days each week, and our Sages in the Talmud tell us that 'a person who keeps fasting is called a sinner.' "

"You are right," said the Rebbe, "I, too, am a sinner. But there is one difference between us. When I sin by fasting, nobody is going to learn from me and try to emulate my ways. When people see you keeping your store open on Shabbos, there may be others who will learn from you and decide to keep their stores open on Shabbos as well."

◦§ Why Bother?

A *rav* in Russia had a son who had abandoned all his religious observances. He even changed his name to Gregory Petrovich, after Peter the Great.

Once, the son came to his father for a Shabbos. He would not go to *shul* with his father — that was outmoded. Nor did he pray alone at home. But he did observe with gusto the *mitzvah* of eating three meals on Shabbos, gobbling down the *kugel* and other delicacies that his mother had made. When he had finished gorging himself, he returned to his room, and after shutting the door smoked a cigarette.

Now the time had come for another *mitzvah* of Shabbos — that of *Sheinah B'Shabbos Ta'anug* — It is a pleasure to sleep on Shabbos — and that, too, he performed scrupulously.

After a long nap, he came into the front of the house, and began arguing with his father about the religious practices of Judaism. "Father," he said, "the problem is that there are so many old-fashioned relics in your observance. What we need is a new Judaism, one in which all types of changes have been introduced. Judaism has to be made more palatable for people."

"That's funny," said his father. "I keep all the *mitzvos*, and I don't find it that hard. Yet you — who have stopped keeping any of the *mitzvos*, who haven't prayed for years, who have not even opened a *sefer* in who knows how long, who enjoys both your mother's *kugel* and the non-Jews' bacon, who has changed his name so as to obliterate any identification with your Judaism — find Judaism too difficult and want to introduce changes in it.

"Let me tell you a story. Once, a man borrowed a considerable sum from another person. As the time for repayment drew near, the borrower became frantic. He simply didn't have the money to pay. Finally, he went over to the lender, poured out his grief, and asked the lender to help him in his hour of need by reducing the amount owed by half.

The lender, a generous man, consented, and they replaced the original IOU with one for half the sum.

"It soon came the time that the payment was due. When the lender asked for his money back, the borrower argued that he owed nothing, and that the IOU held by the lender was forged. 'I don't understand you,' said the lender. 'If you had wanted to claim the IOU was forged, why did you bother to have me write a new note for half the money? You could just as easily have claimed that the original note was forged.'

"And the same is true with you and the other Reformers," concluded his father. "You don't keep even a fraction of the *mitzvos*, yet you claim you want to have our practices changed. What difference would changes make to you anyway? As for us, we wish to keep the entire Torah as it was received from Sinai."

⊰§ *Without Shame*

When the *Ksav Sofer* was the *rav* in Budapest, there was one bank owned by a Jew which kept its doors open on Shabbos. The *Ksav Sofer* tried to persuade him to close his bank on the holy day.

"Rabbi," said the man, "I'm not religious, and I see no reason to close my bank on Shabbos."

"Well, if you won't close your bank because of Fear of Heaven," said the *Ksav Sofer*, "at least do so out of shame."

"What type of shame do you mean?" asked the man. "I'm not ashamed that I'm irreligious."

"You misunderstand me," said the *Ksav Sofer*. "Our Sages tell us that if a person has no shame, that is evidence that his forefathers did not stand at Mount Sinai to receive the Torah. How do we know this? At the time of the giving of the Torah there were no doubts as to who were atheists and who were agnostics. Yet we are told that when they were asked whether they wished to receive the Torah, every single person answered, 'We will do and hearken.' Why did the atheists also answer, 'We will do and hearken?' Because they were ashamed to stand out and not go along with everyone else. Thus, we see that if a person has no shame, it's a sign that his forefathers were not at Sinai."

✑ A Weekday Home

A Reformer once asked R' Azriel Hildesheimer, "Why is it that our temples are always clean and well-kept, while your *shuls* are so old and run-down?"

"The reason," said R' Azriel, "is simple. Your temples are only used on Shabbos and *Yom Tov*, so they always have a Shabbos look about them. Our *shuls*, on the other hand, are used every day, three times a day, and therefore appear much more run-down."

✑ The Right Messenger

R' Zvi Hirsh Berliner was offered the position of *rav* of Berlin, whose Jews had a reputation for being "modern" and not observing the *mitzvos* properly. After much deliberation, R' Zvi Hirsh decided to send someone to visit Berlin and report back to him. At first, he thought of sending a close friend of his who was a great *talmid chacham*, but in the end he sent a man who was himself a bit "modern."

To his friends who were surprised by his choice of emissaries, he explained: "Noah first sent out a raven, and only later did he send the dove. Why? Because if he had sent out the innocent dove, any remaining wicked people would have been able to pull the wool over its eyes and make it think they were righteous. Instead he sent the raven — a non-kosher bird — which would be able to assess the situation accurately.

"Here too, had I sent the *talmid chacham*, the wicked people would have been able to fool him. By sending a person who is somewhat 'modern,' I am confident that those in the 'modern' camp will trust him completely, and this way he will be able to know exactly what the situation is."

~§ Give Credit Where It's Due

A freethinker, who was a major supporter of the drive by the Russian government to force the Jews to abandon their traditional ways, once met R' Eizel Charif. "Rabbi," he said, "I know that you are a vehement opponent of the government. Surely there must be some things about it which you consider positive."

"Indeed that is true," said R' Eizel. "The Russian government has prevented our greatest sages from arguing with one another. In other countries, the sages are often divided up into two camps — those who believe the government is treating the Jews properly and those who disagree with that estimate. In Russia, thank heaven, there is no argument whatsoever among the different sages about this question."

Anti-Semites

◆§ *For the Present-Day Hamans*

R' Yonasan Eybeschuetz was once asked by the non-Jewish mayor of Metz, "Rabbi, since the Torah commands the Jews not to bear a grudge or take revenge, why do you still celebrate Purim and your revenge against Haman?"

"That's not so," answered R' Yonasan. "We don't celebrate Purim because of our revenge against Haman, but as a warning to all present-day Hamans as to the fate that awaits those who attempt to harm the Jews."

◆§ *The Second Haman*

A number of *maskilim* slandered R' Sar Shalom of Belz to the ruling authorities and, consequentially, he was unjustly imprisoned. While in prison, R' Sar Shalom was brought to the district governor to be interrogated. "Listen here," said the governor, "unless you cooperate, all the Jews in the area will suffer. You have found in me a second Haman."

"You should remember," said R' Sar Shalom, "that the first Haman's end was not a particularly happy one."

⋖§ It's All the Jews' Fault!

An anti-Semitic Russian professor once showed a Jewish scholar the work of an apostate Jew in which he quoted *Rashi* as writing, "The place where the Jews lived was the worst of all." "From that you can see," he said, "that even your own scholars agree that wherever there are Jews, the non-Jews living amongst them are worse than non-Jews who have no contact with Jews. It just proves that the Jews are to blame for everything."

"You're absolutely right," the Jewish scholar replied. "Take the Russians as an example. Had there not been any Jews in Russia, they would not have had anyone to kill in their murderous pogroms. Indeed it is the Jews' fault. It is we who give the Russians the opportunity to kill and to maim others."

⋖§ A Question of Perspective

Ignatiev, one of Czar Alexander's ministers, was known as a fanatical anti-Semite. He instituted many decrees designed to make the life of the Jews unbearable. Anti-Semites circulated a rumor that Baron Ginzburg, the richest Jew in Russia, planned to bribe Ignatiev to rescind some of those decrees.

Baron Ginzburg and Ignatiev happened to meet, and Ignatiev commented, "They tell me, Baron, that you plan to bribe me. How much do you intend to pay?"

"That depends," replied Baron Ginzburg. "If you ask me to pay you what *I* think the Jews are worth, I don't have enough with all my assets put together. If, however, you are willing to accept what *you* think the Jews are worth, I am ready to pay you at a moment's notice."

Eretz Yisrael

◄§ A Mother

Thomas Masaryk, president of Czechoslovakia after World
War I, once visited Palestine. During his visit he met with R'
Yosef Chaim Sonnenfeld and became very enthusiastic about
the idea of Jews from all over the world returning to
Palestine. But how could such a small country house so many
people, he wondered.

"King David," R' Yosef Chaim told him, "compared Zion to
a mother. When children return to their mother, she always
has room for them."

◄§ How to Travel to Eretz Yisrael

"There are many people," said R' Nachman of Breslov,
"who would be willing to travel to *Eretz Yisrael* if they could

do so without trouble or expense. The Torah, however, tells us that one who truly wishes to travel to *Eretz Yisrael* must be willing to make whatever sacrifices are necessary, even if it means walking there. This we see from the command of Hashem to Avraham — '*Lech lecha*,' for *lech* literally means walk."

⋙ It Depends on Who Rules

R' Eliyahu Yosef of Drobon became very ill. Nothing that the doctors prescribed seemed to help him. Finally, they resigned themselves to his imminent demise.

R' Eliyahu Yosef heard the prognosis and said to himself, "My illness is exactly like one described in the *Shulchan Aruch* with reference to *treif* animals. Regarding that disease, there is a dispute between R' Yosef Caro, who states that the disease does not render an animal *treif* — i.e., certain to die within one year — and the *Rema*, who says that it does. I will travel to *Eretz Yisrael* where they follow R' Yosef Caro's rulings."

He moved to *Eretz Yisrael* and lived another twenty years.

⋙ No Need to Look for Me

When a noted Rumanian rabbi decided to settle in *Eretz Yisrael*, he was asked why he did not wait for *Mashiach* to bring all Jews to *Eretz Yisrael*.

"When *Mashiach* arrives," answered the *rav*, "I'd rather he found me immediately in Jerusalem rather than have to look for me in Bucharest."

⋙ The Land of Yisrael

R' Yechezkel of Kuzmir once asked a Yerushalmi *rav* why *Eretz Yisrael* is not referred to as *Eretz Avraham* or *Eretz Yitzchak*.

"If it had been named *Eretz Avraham*, Yishmael, too, might claim it, and if it had been named *Eretz Yitzchak*, Esav, too, might lay claim to it. *Eretz Yisrael* means it belongs only to the descendants of Yisrael," the *rav* replied.

"I have a different explanation," said R' Yechezkel. "I think it was named *Eretz Yisrael* because it belongs only to those who act as a *Yisrael* — as a Jew."

⋙ Of Course Hashem Wants It

A native of *Eretz Yisrael* left the country because of the dire poverty there. He prospered in his adopted land, but did not return to *Eretz Yisrael,* despite having enough money to live there comfortably. A visitor from *Eretz Yisrael* once asked him, "*Nu,* R' Meir, when will you be returning to *Eretz Yisrael?*"

The man answered, "*Im yirtzeh Hashem* (literally "if *Hashem* wants it") soon." To this the visitor replied: "Of course *Hashem* wants you to live in *Eretz Yisrael.* Instead what, you should say is *Im yirtzeh R' Meir* — If R' Meir wants it."

⋙ Work — But Not at the Expense of All Else

R' Avraham Yitzchak Kook once toured the new settlements in *Eretz Yisrael.* In most of the settlements, the people had forsaken all *mitzvah* observance.

Rav Kook asked them to explain what they believed in, and they told him, "For two thousand years the Jewish people have been a spiritual nation and have not had the opportunity to work the land. Now we are going to the other extreme, abandoning the world of the spirit, and working the land."

After Rav Kook had heard them out, he said, "I'd like to tell you a story. There was a very wise old man, who forgot everything he had ever learned. To relearn what he had forgotten meant starting again with *aleph-beis.* He was sent to the youngest class where he studied with little children. Soon he also began to join in their childish pranks.

"The teacher called him aside and reminded him, 'It is true that you are studying with little children, but don't forget that you are a respected elder.'

"The same is true here. Ever since we were exiled from our land we have forgotten how to work the land. Now we have to start relearning that skill from scratch. At the same time, we should not forget that we are an ancient and wise nation."

✍§ A Prayer

R' Meir of Premishlan used to quote Yaakov's statement to the shepherds at the well (*Bereishis* 29:3) when he prayed: "Hashem, if the time has not yet come for 'the flocks to be gathered together' — i.e., for all the Jews from around the world to be brought back to *Eretz Yisrael* — at least 'water the sheep and go and feed them' — i.e., ensure that they have enough to keep them alive until *Mashiach* arrives."

✍§ Stones With a Heart

During the 1930's, it was very difficult for Jews to reach the Western Wall because of Arab opposition. Attempts by Jews to pray there often led to riots. Eventually, the British government appointed a commission to investigate the disturbances. One of those called by the commission was R' Avraham Yitzchak Kook. "Rabbi," asked one of the commission members, "what's the big fuss over the Wall? All I see is a bunch of rocks one on top of another."

"Just as there are hearts which are made of stone," replied R' Kook, "so are there stones which have a heart."

✍§ Not to Malign It

R' Yochanan of Rachmistrivka was a great lover of *Eretz Yisrael*. Once he received a bottle of wine from *Eretz Yisrael* but refused to drink it. He explained his refusal simply: "I don't know whether I will like this particular bottle of wine.

Since I don't want, Heaven forbid, to possibly disparage something from *Eretz Yisrael,* I would rather not drink the wine."

✒ Jerusalem Didn't Like You

A certain chassid moved from Poland to *Eretz Yisrael* and settled in Jerusalem. After having lived in the city for about a year, he decided that he couldn't adapt to the life-style in the country, and decided to return to Poland.

Before leaving *Eretz Yisrael*, he went to R' Simchah Bunim of Worka, to bid him farewell and to receive his blessing for his return trip.

R' Simchah Bunim sighed a long sigh, from the depths of his heart, and told the chassid, "I really pity you. Jerusalem evidently didn't like you. Had Jerusalem liked you, you would have liked Jerusalem."

A short time later the chassid returned to R' Simchah Bunim to tell him that he had decided to stay after all.

Books and Authors

✍§ A Real Chiddush

R' Yosef Rozhin, the Rogachover Gaon, gave very few *haskamos* (letters of approbation) to authors who sent or brought their works to him. An author once brought him a *sefer* which had been printed in Grayova. The Rogachover took the *sefer*, turned a few pages, and told the man, "I've really learned something new."

"What is it?" the author asked excitedly.

"I never knew there was a printing press in Grayova," replied the Rogachover.

His Words Are Worth a Thousand Pictures

When the Sochachover Rebbe, the author of *Avnei Nezer*, was in Warsaw, he stayed at the home of one of his wealthy chassidim. As his host was showing him around the house, he pointed to a painting and told the Sochachover that it was a painting of the *Baal HaTanya*.

"A person who learns the *Tanya* knows what he looks like, without needing to see a picture," countered the Sochachover.

It's Not the Same Thing

A famous *maggid* was known far and wide for the impact of his words of rebuke. After his death, all his sermons were published, but for some reason they had little effect on readers. Yet those who had heard the *maggid* attested that the content was identical. What was missing, they decided, was the deep sighs, coming from the heart, with which the *maggid* punctuated his sermons.

It's the Contents Which Count

A man came to R' Eizel Charif to ask for his *haskamah* — endorsement — on a volume he had written. As they spoke, the man tried to impress R' Eizel with his *yichus* — (ancestry).

"Let me tell you something," said R' Eizel. "*Shir HaShirim* begins, 'The Songs of Songs, of Shlomo.' We are told no more about the author, and yet R' Akiva stated that if the other books are holy, the Song of Songs is the holy of holies.' On the other hand, the Book of *Koheles*, also by Shlomo, gives much more of his *yichus* — 'The words of *Koheles* son of David, king in Yerushalayim' — and yet we are told that the Sages considered leaving it out of *Tanach*. From this we see that *yichus* is entirely irrelevant when it comes to a *haskamah*."

◆§ Like the Malbim

An author brought a commentary he had written on *Koheles* to R' Eizel Charif for his *haskamah*. As he read through some of the pages, R' Eizel exclaimed, "Exactly the same method as the *Malbim*." Nevertheless, he refused to give a *haskamah* to the work.

"Why not?" asked the man. "After all, you yourself said that it's exactly the same method as the *Malbim*."

"That's exactly the problem," said R' Eizel. "You see, where *Chazal* tell us that Achashverosh was a fool, the *Malbim* goes to great lengths to show he was a wise man. We are told that Shlomo was the wisest of all men, but your commentary would make him out to be the opposite!"

◆§ Walking the Path of the Righteous

The Gaon of Vilna used to say, "There are many *sefarim* which are greater than their author. In the case of the ethical work, *Mesilas Yesharim*, on the other hand, one can immediately see that the author was greater than the *sefer*. Had the author been alive today, I would have been willing to walk as far as necessary to hear him."

◆§ The Opposite Would Have Been More Appropriate

A wealthy and learned Jew once told the *Chafetz Chaim* that he had bequeathed his extensive Torah library to various yeshivos. "And how about your assets?" asked the *Chafetz Chaim*. The man replied that he had left his money to his sons. "Well then," persisted the *Chafetz Chaim*, "why didn't you leave them your library?" The man explained that his sons were all successful businessmen and didn't have time to study Torah.

"You would have done much better," said the *Chafetz Chaim*, "if you had reversed the conditions of your will. Your sons are businessmen in their own right and don't need your money. On the other hand, the yeshivos are in desperate need of money. As for your library, the yeshivos all have libraries. It is your sons who need the *sefarim* in your library. Perhaps one day they will look at the *sefarim* and begin to learn Torah."

◦§ The Beautiful Sefer Torah

A *sofer* brought a *Sefer Torah* which he had written to R' Zvi Elimelech of Dinov, to show him the beautiful calligraphy. "Indeed, the writing is very nice," said R' Zvi Elimelech, "but the contents are absolutely phenomenal!"

◦§ At Least One Item

A chassid of the Gerrer Rebbe, R' Avraham Mordechai, once came to see the Rebbe. He was fascinated by the Rebbe's library, which consisted of thousands of volumes, and thought to himself, "How can anyone ever have time to learn so many volumes?" At that moment, the Rebbe walked in, saw him looking around, and said, "One doesn't have to read every single volume in his library, but one should at least know one thought from each volume."

Jewish Thought

Aphorisms

R' Aharon of Karlin would say:

We ask Hashem in our prayers, "Build it [the *Beis HaMikdash*] speedily in our days." If we use our days wisely, without wasting them, we contribute to the building of the *Beis HaMikdash.*

The *halachah* is that a person who reads the *megillah* backwards has not fulfilled his obligation. A person who regards the miracle of the *megillah* as having happened "backwards" — i.e., in the past — but not in our day, has not fulfilled his obligation.

A person who refrains from sin, even if it is only from pity on himself — i.e., out of a desire to avoid punishment — is considered a good person.

❦   ❦   ❦

R' Akiva Eiger would say:

Just as a person exerts himself to ensure that he has a proper quantity of wine for the *Seder*, so should he exert himself to ensure that he has a proper quantity of *maror*.

❀ ❀ ❀

R' Boruch Ber Leibowitz would say:

Any day I do not come up with a new *chiddush*, I literally feel sick.

❀ ❀ ❀

R' Chaim of Volozhin would say:

A person accomplishes much more through patience than with all the anger in the world.

❀ ❀ ❀

R' David Moshe of Chortkov would say:

There are seventy facets to the Torah: One of these is that silence is a retaining wall to preserve knowledge.

❀ ❀ ❀

R' David of Novaodok would say:

Why is it that a person does not have what he wants? It is because he does not want what he has. If he wanted only what he has, he would have what he wants.

❀ ❀ ❀

R' Levi Yitzchak of Berdichev would say:

A person who allows pride into his heart is guilty of the sin, "You shall not bring an abomination into your home," for there is no greater abomination than pride.

❀ ❀ ❀

R' Meir Shapiro of Lublin would say:

There are those who hear the blowing of the *shofar* throughout the year.

A Jew sometimes forgets that Hashem, too, can help him.

✿ ✿ ✿

R' Menachem Mendel of Kotzk would say:

To permit a fool to have his say without contradicting him is also in the category of *gemilas chassadim* — helping one's fellow man.

Whoever does not see Hashem everywhere does not see Him anywhere.

Not only is a person who hates another wicked, but a person who hates himself is also considered wicked.

The greatest cry is when a person needs to weep but is unable to do so.

A person must always be careful of three things: not to look outside of himself, not to look inside his fellow, and not to think of himself.

✿ ✿ ✿

R' Menachem Mendel of Lubavitch would say:

The worst of all conceits is the conceit that one is a pious individual.

✿ ✿ ✿

R' Menachem Mendel of Vitebsk would say:

True fear of sin is fearing the sin itself more than its punishment.

✿ ✿ ✿

R' Mendele of Kosov would say:

When I address the people and speak words of rebuke, I am not thinking of anyone in particular. But if anyone thinks that I mean him, then indeed I am speaking to him directly.

✿ ✿ ✿

R' Moshe Leib of Sassov would say:

I and eight others like me cannot form a *minyan*, yet ten simple tailors constitute a *minyan*.

A person attains a higher level of piety by conquering his anger than he would by fasting a thousand days.

❀ ❀ ❀

R' Moshe of Kobrin would say:
When a person suffers, he should not say that things are bad, but rather that they are bitter. Some medicines are very bitter.

❀ ❀ ❀

R' Naftali of Ropshitz would say:
A Jew must always look toward Heaven, while remaining on earth. He must remember Heaven but stand on the ground.

❀ ❀ ❀

R' Pinchas of Koretz would say:
It is your duty to serve Hashem as if you were the only person in the entire world.
If a person's prayer is not said on behalf of the entire Jewish people, it is not a prayer.
Falsehood has become so much a part of our daily lives that no sooner does a person wake up in the morning and open his mouth than a lie jumps out.
If you wish to love the truth, start by hating falsehood. From that, you will automatically come to love the truth.

❀ ❀ ❀

R' Shmelke of Nikolsburg would say:
More than the poor man needs alms, those who are able need poor men to whom to give. More than those without a place to eat need a home into which to be invited, those with homes require a poor person to invite.

❀ ❀ ❀

R' Simchah Bunim of Pshischa would say:
A humble person removes pride from his heart, and the resulting vacuum is then filled with love of Hashem.

It is far worse for a person not to do *teshuvah* for a sin than to commit the sin in the first place. When one commits a sin, the offense is for but a short duration, while every moment one does not repent is another sin.

❁ ❁ ❁

R' Wolf of Strikov would say:
To understand a foreign language requires only a year or two of study; but to understand one's own language, even seventy years is too short.

❁ ❁ ❁

R' Yaakov Yosef of Polnoye would say:
If a person does not appreciate himself, how can he possibly appreciate others?

❁ ❁ ❁

R' Yechiel Michel of Zlotchov would say:
There are two things one is not allowed to worry about: those things which can be fixed and those which cannot. If they can be fixed, then fix them rather than worrying. If they cannot be fixed, what purpose does worrying serve?

❁ ❁ ❁

R' Yerucham Levovitz would say:
If a man tells me that he is unable to study Torah because he does not have any *sefarim* available to him, I am simply unable to remain in his presence. Hashem gave you a mind. Think!

❁ ❁ ❁

R' Yisrael Salanter would say:
A person has to spend his time ensuring that nothing breaks. The repairs will then take care of themselves.
One who works for the community must have three qualities: He must not tire, he must not become angry, and he must not long to have the work completed.

Had Yom Kippur come but once every seventy years, at which time one's sins would be forgiven, that would have been a source of very great joy for us. Now that we have Yom Kippur every year, how much greater is our joy.

❧ ❧ ❧

R' Yitzchak Blaser would say:
The *yetzer hara* is like a fly. Even though one constantly chases it away, it keeps returning.

❧ ❧ ❧

R' Yitzchak Meir of Gur would say:
It is more important for me to do what Hashem wants than for Hashem to do what I want.

❧ ❧ ❧

R' Yosef Yozel Horowitz of Novarodok would say:
A yeshivah is not measured by how many good students and how many bad students it contains, but by how it defines "good" and "bad."

❧ ❧ ❧

R' Ze'ev of Strikov would say:
If a person does not want to give *tzedakah* — "charity" — he does not have to give any. He has no right, however, to rob the poor man of his poverty by claiming that he is not worthy of receiving *tzedakah*.

❧ ❧ ❧

R' Zev Wolf of Zhitomir would say:
Rather than worrying about what to do tomorrow, rectify that which you did yesterday.

❧ ❧ ❧

R' Zvi Hirsh of Zidichov would say:
Those who claim that there is no one except their rebbe in the entire world are guilty of idolatry. The fact is that

every rebbe is right for his disciples, and our rebbe is right for us.

❀ ❀ ❀

Maggid of Kuznitz would say:
A person who claims to fast from Sunday to Friday, while secretly eating at night, is fooling the world. One who does fast from Sunday to Friday is fooling himself.

❀ ❀ ❀

Maggid of Mezritch would say:
Before he prays, a Jew should tell himself that he is ready to die with that prayer.
It is a great mercy of Hashem that one remains alive after reciting his prayers; by all logic he should have died, having drained all his strength during his prayers.

❀ ❀ ❀

Noam Megadim would say:
When we are told, "Love your neighbor as yourself," it means exactly that. It does not mean that you should love him more than yourself, by expecting him to be a better person than you or to fear Hashem more than you, and then being upset at him when he is not better than you.

❀ ❀ ❀

Baal Shem Tov would say:
Every person sometimes has the urge to do *teshuvah*, but some people drown that urge in liquor.
Whoever worries about the World-to-Come has both this world and the World-to-Come; whoever worries about this world has neither this world nor the World-to-Come.
A Jew can never be alone. Wherever he is, Hashem is with him.
When the Jewish people suffer in any way, the suffering comes in order to improve them and make them better. Our suffering is likened to a father chastising his son in order to

have him follow the correct path. The father, however, suffers more than the child when he must chastise him.

❦ ❦ ❦

Chafetz Chaim would say:
Everyone worries that he does not have enough to live. Why do people not worry that they might not have enough to die?

❦ ❦ ❦

Chozeh of Lublin would say:
It is possible for a person to spend his whole life fasting and afflicting himself and yet not fear Hashem.

◆§ Sayings of the Ba'alei Mussar

A person is not upset about the fact that he lacks intelligence, but about the fact that others say that he lacks intelligence.

When a wise man makes a mistake, he blames himself. When a fool makes a mistake, he blames others.

A wise man knows that his intelligence is limited, while a fool thinks he knows everything.

◆§ Sayings of the Lubavitcher Chassidim

"You shall love Hashem your God" is not only a command, but also a promise.

A house is built with wisdom and not with tools.

A person must respect his own body as much as he respects his fellow's body.

If a Jew walks on the road without thinking Torah thoughts, each stone on which he treads says to him, "Who gave you permission to step on me?"

Intellect by itself is a head without a body.

It is better to eat in order to pray than to pray in order to eat.

It is easier to rectify one's deeds than to rectify one's thoughts.

It is not enough to understand the meaning of the prayers. One must *feel* their meaning.

Man's primary purpose is to transform his bodily functions into a service of Hashem.

Not everything which is permitted is truly permitted.

One must love one's fellow Jew as he acts in the synagogue, and not as he acts at home.

People become so used to the dark that they think it is light.

The service of Hashem begins with the morning prayer "*Modeh ani* — I thank" Hashem.

To Hashem, every Jew is an only child.

◄§ Sayings of R' Nachman of Breslov

A person who is a believer but who has no knowledge can fall, but one who believes and has knowledge cannot fall.

A simple person will eat in order to have the strength to learn, but one on a higher level will learn in order to know how to eat.

Each day a person is that much closer to death. How can he have time for arguments?

Passing through this world involves walking on a very narrow bridge, and the most important thing is not to fear.

One can evaluate a country by the jokes which circulate there.

The desire to do good is itself good.

The soul of each Jew, be he the least worthy of all, is strong enough to withstand all the temptations of this world.

There are many doors which lead out of the darkness, but man is blind.

By the way a person sings a *niggun*, one can tell if he has accepted upon himself the yoke of Heaven.

Many people cry when they are in financial distress, but few cry when they are in spiritual distress — when they have sinned. Woe to people who cry for all the wrong reasons.

Every person is a mixture of the "four sons" mentioned in the *Haggadah.* Fortunate is the person in whom the wise son controls the others.

Speaking *lashon hara* is no less a sin than eating non-kosher food. Just as one must ask a *rav* before eating something questionable, one must ask a *rav* before saying something questionable.

One must rejoice in the performance of a *mitzvah* until he desires nothing more than the opportunity to perform another *mitzvah*.

~§ *Unattributed Sayings*

All the world is a burning bush, but only those with eyes take off their shoes.

An hour devoted by a mother to her children is worth ten hours devoted by others.

Children must be taught to listen to their parents, but parents must also be taught to listen to what bothers their children.

False modesty is true conceit.

Not to believe *lashon hara* is even harder than not to speak *lashon hara*.

One can transgress the law of *lashon hara* with only a smile, a wink, or even silence.

One should see his own faults through a magnifying lens and the faults of others through a lens which reduces their size.

We are told that "Torah weakens one's power" — it weakens one's power to sin.

When children are not taught to obey their parents, in the end the parents will obey their children.

You do not have to believe what a person says about himself. You are *forbidden* to believe what he says about others.

⋅§ A Kemeiyah That Worked

R' Yechezkel Landau, the *Noda B'Yehudah*, was totally opposed to the use of *kemeiyot* — kabbalistic texts written on parchment for the purpose of protecting or curing the wearer. Only once did he violate his rule never to give *kemeiyot*. A woman in Prague, where he was the *rav*, became convinced that she was mortally ill and only a *kemeiyah* from R' Yechezkel would cure her. The doctors could find nothing wrong with her, yet the woman wasted away day by day.

Finally, her husband came to R' Yechezkel and begged him to make an exception to his rule against writing *kemeiyot*. R' Yechezkel agreed and entered his private chambers where he took a piece of blank parchment, rolled it up in cloth, and brought it out to the waiting husband. "Tell your wife she is to wear this on a chain around her neck for thirty days," he told the husband. "After thirty days, she is to take off the *kemeiyah* and unwrap it. If the writing on the parchment has vanished, she may rest assured that she has been cured."

The woman did as instructed, and when she unwrapped the parchment thirty days later, she found it was blank. She soon made a full recovery.

~§ Don't Be an Example to Others!

R' Gershon Hanoch of Radzin once had a dentist pull an aching tooth. As the dentist was about to leave, R' Gershon Hanoch asked him for a bill.

"Rebbe," said the dentist, "since it's Chanukah right now, and I would normally have brought you a donation for Chanukah, let's consider my services in place of the money I would have brought you."

"That's fine," said the Rebbe, "provided you don't tell my chassidim about it. I wouldn't want others to decide that instead of bringing me a donation, they'll pull out one of my teeth!"

~§ A Threat

Two men brought a *din Torah* before R' Menachem Mendel of Linsk. After R' Menachem Mendel rendered his judgment, the losing party refused to accept it. Seeing this, R' Menachem Mendel glared at the man and told him, "I want you to know that high in my room, above all the boxes, I have a special box filled with anger. If you force me to, I will climb up there and take out some of that anger. If I do, you'll be struck with an incurable disease." Hearing this, the man's face went pale, and he promised to abide by the verdict.

~§ In the Flesh

Emperor Franz Josef of Austria once visited the Great Synagogue in Cracow, which contained a portrait of the emperor.

That day, however, someone had removed the portrait in order to discredit the Jewish community in the emperor's eyes. The emperor was told that the picture had been removed by the Jews as a protest against him.

When the emperor entered the Great Synagogue he looked around and saw no portrait of himself. He then asked the *rav*, R' Shimon Sofer, whether it was true that a picture of himself had been removed prior to his arrival.

R' Shimon, who had only learned of the painting's removal at that moment, did not lose his composure for an instant. He told the emperor, "Your majesty, you are absolutely right. Let me explain. Throughout the week, we place black boxes with leather straps on our arms and heads when we pray in the morning, in order to bind ourselves symbolically to G-d. On Saturdays, however, we feel so close to G-d that we feel no need for any such symbol and do not wear the black boxes.

"The same is true here, your majesty," he continued. "Throughout the year we have a portrait of you on the wall to remind us of you. But to leave such a painting on the wall when you are with us is unnecessary, and we therefore removed the picture in anticipation of your visit."

⟊ *When to Fear*

The *Chiddushei HaRim* was traveling in a horse-drawn coach when the horses suddenly began to gallop down a steep incline. Everyone in the coach, except for the *Chiddushei HaRim*, was terrified.

When they finally came to a level stretch, one of the other passengers asked the *Chiddushei HaRim* why he hadn't been frightened. The *Chiddushei HaRim* told him, "When a person is constantly aware of the danger of succumbing to the *yetzer hara*, which confronts him every minute of the day, no external event can frighten him."

Impeccable Logic

✍§ A Good Advocate

The *Chafetz Chaim* once bemoaned the fact that so many Jews had stopped keeping *mitzvos*, and those who still observed *mitzvos* did so without any strong conviction.

R' Naftali Trop, one of the *roshei yeshivah* in the Radin Yeshiva, told him, "I am not at all surprised. Look at what happened in Egypt. The Jews sank to the depths of impurity there, even though they were only a few generations removed from Avraham, Yitzchak, and Yaakov. Yet our generation is thousands of years removed from our forefathers and we suffer like our ancestors in Egypt. Is it surprising then that so many of our brothers have drifted away?"

The *Chafetz Chaim* was very pleased with his words, and told him, "You are a fine advocate for the Jewish people. Your words will undoubtedly rise to Hashem's Throne of Glory."

⊷ A Little Humility, Please!

A young man came to his rebbe and complained, "Rebbe, what can I do about my pride? I simply can't overcome it." "Sit by me today, my son," said the rebbe, "and just remain quiet."

Soon, a man came in to the rebbe with a request. "Rebbe, help me," he said. "My daughter has the chance of marrying an exceptional young man, but I need money for her dowry. Without that money, the *shidduch* will be called off."

"Young man," asked the rebbe, turning to him, "would you by any chance have a few thousand dollars to lend?"

"Rebbe," said the young man, "I'm destitute. I barely survive. There is no way I could loan such a sum."

The rebbe then lent the man money.

A short while later, a butcher came in. "Rebbe," he said, "I've slaughtered a bull, and I found some questionable marks on the lungs. Is the meat kosher or not?"

"Young man," said the rebbe, "you've seen the lungs. What is your decision?"

"Rebbe," replied the young man, "I don't know enough to render a verdict."

Later, one of the leading merchants of the city came in. "Rebbe," he begged, "you've got to help me. I entered into a business deal with the local baron, and I don't know what to do. Please advise me."

"Young man," said the rebbe again, "what would you suggest?"

"Rebbe, I've no idea," answered the young man. "I've never been in business in my life."

After the merchant left, the rebbe turned to the young man again and said to him, "My son, I really don't understand you.

You don't have any money to your name, you don't know the first thing about *halachah*, and you have no inkling about business. What can you possibly find to be proud about?"

~§ A Little Too Glib

Yosef Shor, a pious Jew, was appointed by the Austrian government to serve as a judge in Tarnapol. One day, a Jew was accused of having deliberately set a fire, with the intention of burning down the whole town. The prosecution brought five non-Jewish witnesses. Each stated clearly that he had been present when the Jew had lit the fire. The defense attorney could not shake their testimony in any way. Throughout the case, Yosef Shor did not utter a word.

As the judges deliberated the case, Yosef Shor still remained silent. Finally, the time came for the judges to vote. All the other judges voted guilty, while Yosef Shor voted innocent.

"I don't understand," said one of the other judges. "How can you vote to acquit this man when all the evidence is against him?"

"You're wrong, my dear colleague," said Yosef Shor. "All the evidence here is fabricated. Can you imagine that these five burly witnesses saw this weak, little Jew lighting a fire in the middle of the town and stood by doing nothing to prevent him from doing so?"

The police investigated further, and found that the five "witnesses" had indeed been lying.

~§ A Simple Test

A few hundred years ago, it was the custom for boys and girls to be married off at a very young age. When R' Yechezkel Landau, the *Noda B'Yehudah*, served as the *rav* in Prague, he officiated at the marriage of the daughter of one of the leading merchants of the city to a boy of only thirteen who was considered a brilliant young scholar. For half a year the couple lived happily, but then they began to quarrel. One day, still in their first year of marriage, the young man picked himself up and vanished from the city. Of course his young bride was left all alone, unable to marry anyone else.

About five years later, a young man with a beard entered the main *shul* in Prague, took out a *sefer*, and began learning. He seemed to know his way around the *shul*. Several of the congregants noticed a resemblance to the groom who had disappeared years ago. Finally, they brought the wife's father and the wife herself to look at the young man, and indeed there was a strong resemblance.

They hurried to R' Yechezkel, and told him that they thought the husband had returned. Without delay, he had the young man brought to him and questioned him. Finally the young man broke down and admitted that he was indeed the missing husband. When asked for proof of his claim, he mentioned various facts and incidents that only the husband himself could have known. There was only one problem — in spite of his confession, the young woman was still not totally convinced that this was indeed her husband. Something was amiss.

Finally, R' Yechezkel gave his verdict. He declared that the husband had indeed returned. For the first week, however, the husband and wife were to live apart. Privately, R' Yechezkel told the wife's father that he wanted to test the young man one final time. When the young man and the wife's father went to *shul* on Friday night, the wife's father was to stop to talk to the *shamash* at the *shul* door and send the young man ahead to sit down.

During that week, the wife's father had the young man come to the family table, where he treated him royally. On Friday evening, as arranged, the young man accompanied the wife's father to the main *shul*, where he *davened* only on Shabbos. Pausing at the door to speak to the *shamash*, the wife's father told the young man, "I have something to discuss right now. Go sit next to where I normally sit." The young man had no choice but to go ahead on his own. It soon became clear that he had no idea where to sit.

After Shabbos, R' Yechezkel summoned the young man to him. Confronted with the evidence, he admitted that he had befriended the husband and had taken advantage of his innocence to learn all types of personal details from him. Then, relying on the fact that he looked somewhat like the husband, he had tried to fool everyone into believing that he was indeed the son-in-law of the wealthy merchant.

R' Yechezkel explained later that he had sensed that the young man was an imposter, despite his wealth of information about the wife and her family. Therefore he had to devise a test involving the type of information which he would have never thought to obtain, such as where his father-in-law sat in *shul.*

⋅⋅⋅§ *A Logical Question*

R' Avraham of Porisov saw a young man pacing back and forth in the *beis medrash*. He called him over and said to him: "Young man, I don't understand you. First you started in one corner. You obviously didn't like it and thought the other corner might be better. So you paced across the room. After you got there, you realized that the first corner was better after all, so you returned to it. What I don't understand is why you then returned to the second corner, which you had already found to be worse than the first!"

⋅⋅⋅§ *A Question of Perspective*

R' Yonasan Eybeschuetz was once summoned to the office of the governor of Prague to meet with the city officials. R' Yonasan came to the meeting elegantly dressed. One of the local officials, who considered himself an expert on Jewish law, reproached him: "Rabbi," he said, "aren't you violating the statement in *Mishlei* (25:6), that one must not adorn himself in the presence of a king? Furthermore, the *Gemara* states (*Chagigah* 9) that 'poverty becomes Israel,' and you are dressed like a rich man.'"

Without a pause, R' Yonasan answered, "Actually, your two questions answer one another. Since one is not allowed to adorn himself in the presence of a king, I had to be sure to wear clothes that are not considered an adornment. Now, which clothes are considered an adornment for Jews? This we learn from the *Gemara* — the clothes of the poor are the Jews' adornment. I was thus forced to wear elegant clothing when appearing before the governor."

⋖§ A Small Loan, Please

An itinerant *maggid* was once addressing a congregation. In his *derashah* he mentioned that the World-to-Come will be the exact opposite of this world. "In the next world," he said, "those who are poor will be rich, and those who are rich will be poor."

After his *derashah* a man came over to him and said, "Rabbi, I am destitute. Does that mean that in the World-to-Come I will be wealthy?" The *maggid* replied that that would be the case.

"Well then," said the man, "could you please lend me enough money to open a business? I will pay you back in the World-to-Come."

"There's only one problem with your logic, my son," said the *maggid*. "If I lend you money now, and your business prospers, as you hope, you'll be wealthy in this world. That means that you will be poor in the World-to-Come. How, then, will you be able to repay me?"

⋖§ Addressing the Common Man

When R' Shmelke became rabbi of Nikolsburg, his first *derashah* showed his wide-ranging knowledge of what was happening in the world, as well as his great erudition in Torah. When he was asked later why he had injected so much secular knowledge into his *derashah*, he replied, "That a *rav* is expected to know Torah is obvious. But many of the unlearned people in town believe that the *rav* knows only Torah and nothing else, and that it is therefore pointless to talk to him of their daily affairs. They reject any rebuke for it comes from someone out of touch with daily life. I therefore felt it was important for my new congregants to see that I am very much aware of what goes on in the world."

ᴥᦥ *All for Peace*

R' Chaim Brisker once became involved in trying to make peace between two simple men. One of those close to him asked, "Rebbe, is it fitting for someone of your stature to become involved in such petty matters?"

R' Chaim answered, "The *halachah* states that at the end of the *Shemoneh Esrei* one must take three steps back before he is allowed to say '*Shalom.*' For *shalom*, peace, it is worth taking a few steps back."

ᴥᦥ *An Oath of a Different Kind*

A wealthy man and his servant brought a large shipment of wine to Prague to be sold at the local fair. Before they left home, the servant, who had saved a little money, placed it in a bag. He then hid the bag in one of barrels and specially marked the barrel.

When they arrived in Prague, the servant opened the marked barrel, but to his horror the money was gone. He searched frantically, but the money was nowhere to be found. In desperation, he approached his master, who knew where the money had been hidden, and asked if he knew anything about its disappearance. His master became furious and screamed, "What? You think I took your money? Away with you!"

With no other choice, the servant went to the *Noda B'Yehudah*, the *rav* of Prague, and told him the entire story. The *Noda B'Yehudah* summoned the master, who denied any knowledge of the money. "If that is the case," said the *Noda*

B'Yehudah, "there is only one other possible explanation — one of the non-Jews at the inn where you stayed on your journey must have searched all the barrels to find the purse. All your wine is now *yayin nesech* and may not be used by Jews."

Realizing that he stood to lose his entire fortune, the merchant broke down and confessed that he had stolen his poor servant's money. The *Noda B'Yehudah*, however, refused to believe him and accused him of only trying to protect his investment. The merchant begged the *Noda B'Yehudah* to believe him, and even offered proof that he, indeed, had stolen the money. Finally, the *Noda B'Yehudah* agreed to accept the man's word if he took a public oath that he had stolen the money and returned it, along with a substantial penalty, to his poor servant.

◆§ Ask Your Local Rav

R' Abele Posviller of Vilna was once talking in learning with his students when a distraught servant girl walked in. R' Abele immediately stopped the discussion and asked her what he could do to help her.

"Rabbi," she replied, "please tell me what I should prepare for my mistress' lunch today."

"My child, prepare noodles," he told her.

After she had left, R' Abele explained to his students what had happened. The maid must have asked her mistress what to prepare for lunch, and her mistress answered angrily, "How should I know? Go and ask the *rav!*"

"That was why she came to me," concluded R' Abele.

◆§ Crowing Loudly

When the Dubno *Maggid* moved into a certain town, the local *rav* was very upset. "The people barely pay me a living wage," he said, "and now with two of us here, we'll both starve."

The Dubno *Maggid* told him a *mashal*: "A farmer had a hen, which he often forgot to feed. One day, the man brought in a rooster. 'Now we'll definitely starve to death,' moaned the hen to the rooster. 'I can barely survive on what I get.'

" 'On the contrary,' said the rooster. 'With me here, you'll eat more than you ever did before. I'll keep crowing, and the man will never again forget to feed us.'

"By the same token," said the Dubno Maggid, "my presence will draw the attention of the people to both of us, so that your situation will only improve."

ҙ Even in the Midst of War

In the midst of one of the wars fought between France and Austria, two Jews were arrested in Pressburg on charges of selling arms to the enemy. After a summary court martial, they were sentenced to death.

When the *Chasam Sofer* heard of this, he went to see Prince Carl, the commander-in-chief of the Austrian forces, and begged him to give the Jews a full and fair trial. "Otherwise," he said, "you may well be executing two completely innocent people."

"First of all," said the prince, "the two are certainly not completely innocent. Second, even if they are innocent of this charge, in wartime there are thousands of innocent people who are killed. That's the nature of war. We simply don't have time to conduct a full trial at a critical time like this."

"Your highness," said the *Chasam Sofer*, "in the Bible we are taught the laws concerning the investigations the elders of a city must make if a murdered man is found nearest to their city. This particular section the Bible is preceded and followed by accounts of military ventures, to teach us that, even in the midst of battle, justice must be done."

✑ Hashem Still Is One

In Lemberg there was a dishonest Jewish judge, who nevertheless prayed with great devotion. He used to linger especially long over the word "One" in the *Shema*. R' Yaakov Orenstein, the *rav* of the town, explained that the judge's piety was perfectly appropriate: "*Chazal* tell us that a judge who judges honestly is considered to be a partner with Hashem. This judge, however, wishes to assure us that he is in no sense entering into a partnership with Hashem, and that Hashem still remains One."

✑ Head Covering

A non-religious man once walked through Me'ah She'arim. A little boy asked him where his *yarmulke* was. Pointing towards the sky, the man said, "Up there — it's a big, blue hat."

"What a big hat for such a small head," commented the little boy.

✑ How Many Masters Does One Need?

R' Avraham of Chichnov was offered the position of *rav* of Lublin. He turned down the offer, commenting, "Why should I leave Chichnov, where I am the servant of thousands of Jews, and move to Lublin, where I'll be the servant of tens of thousands of Jews?"

✑ No Favoritism at All

A chassid once accused R' Avraham Yaakov of Sadigura of favoring his wealthy followers: "When a poor man walks into your study, he's in and out in a very short time, while the rich remain with you for much longer periods."

R' Avraham Yaakov told his chassid that he was mistaken as to the reason the rich stayed longer: "When a poor man comes in to me, he knows exactly what he is lacking and what he wants from me. Yet, I have to speak to a wealthy man at length until he realizes what it is he is lacking."

⊷ Not Because I Want to

The Dubno *Maggid* once went wandering from town to town to earn money to support his family. In each place he would preach and receive a small sum of money in return.

At one of his first stops, the communal leaders asked him, "Rabbi, if you are so desperately in need of money, why didn't you stay and preach in Dubno where everyone knows you, rather than wander about to towns where people have not really heard of you? Wouldn't you do better financially in Dubno?"

"Our sages tell us," the Dubno *Maggid* replied, "that when Rivkah was pregnant with Yaakov and Esav, she was in great agony. Whenever she passed the *beis medrash* of Shem and Ever, Yaakov pushed to leave the womb, and when she passed temples of idolatry, Esav struggled to go out. This seems strange. Couldn't Rivkah have spared herself from all of this discomfort by simply staying at home? From this we learn that Rivkah walked about not because she wanted to, but because she knew that if she remained at home and did nothing, she would be even worse off."

⊷ Only a Little Dirt

R' Yonasan Eybeschuetz was extremely quick witted, and was often asked by non-Jews for explanations of various Jewish laws and customs. A gentile official once asked him, "You Jews are so intelligent. Why, then, do you believe in a religion which is so illogical? If a chicken eats a pound of butter and is then slaughtered properly, you will eat it without any qualms. But if a dab of butter falls into a pot in which that same chicken is being cooked, you will not touch it."

"The truth is," R' Yonasan replied, "that you act no differently. If a pig wallows in all the dirt and filth in the world, it can be slaughtered and served at the fanciest of banquets. But let just a little of that filth fall into the pot where the pig is being cooked, and the dish is no longer considered fit for anything."

◁§ Qualities of a Rebbe

The *Yehudi Hakadosh* explained *Chazal*'s statement that "one who walks to the right of his rebbe is a boor" as follows: "*Chazal* tell us that a rebbe's left hand should push one away, while his right hand should draw closer. One who seeks a rebbe who only uses the 'right hand' — i.e., a rebbe who only draws him closer without ever rebuking him — is indeed a boor."

◁§ Regardless

The Baal Shem Tov taught: "There are three *mitzvos* which are worthwhile, even if one performed them without having the proper intention: Torah study — because regardless of one's intention, he has acquired greater Torah knowledge; *tzedakah* — because the poor have benefited; and *mikveh* — because one emerges *tahor* (purified)."

◁§ The Blessing of a Kohen to a Kohen

When R' Yitzchak Elchanan Spektor turned seventy-five, all the great Torah authorities sent him messages of congratulation, including R' Shlomo HaKohen of Vilna. His message was but three Hebrew words long: "*Birkas Kohen leKohen*" — the blessing of a *Kohen* to a *Kohen*. When the message was read aloud, those present were amazed, for R' Yitzchak was not a *Kohen*. Seeing their amazement, R' Yitzchak explained, "I'm surprised at you. The word '*Kohen*' in *gematria* — its numerical value — is seventy-five. R' Shlomo simply wrote,

'The greetings of a *Kohen* to a person reaching seventy -five.' "

⋙ The Heavier the Better

The *Chafetz Chaim* used to tell the following parable: "When a peddler goes out on a trip, he carries as large a load as he can, for the more he carries, the more he has available to sell. We should do the same on our journey through life. The greater the burden one carries in this world, in terms of Torah study and the observance of the other *mitzvos*, the greater will be one's 'profit' in the World-to-Come. Only a fool lightens his 'baggage' in this world, ignoring the 'profit' of the World-to-Come."

⋙ The Pot Must Be Kosher as Well

A certain *maggid* came to Brisk and asked permission to preach. Inasmuch as he was not known for his piety, R' Chaim of Brisk refused to allow him to speak. The *maggid* begged R' Chaim to reconsider. His speeches, the man said, were based solely on sacred texts, without any addition on his part; so why should he be denied the opportunity to earn a little money through his preaching?

R' Chaim replied, "If a kosher animal is properly slaughtered, and nothing is found wrong with its lungs and the meat is kashered properly, then it is kosher. Nevertheless, if that meat is cooked in a non-kosher pot, it becomes *treif*."

⋙ Vengeance Is Mine

A priest once said to R' Zzvi Hirsh Charif of Halberstadt, "You have to admit one thing: We Christians have more love than you do. After all, ours is a G-d of love, whereas yours is the G-d of vengeance."

"The opposite is true," replied R' Zvi Hirsh. "Since we see G-d as the G-d of vengeance, we leave all vengeance to Him, while we are commanded to love others. You, however, view Him as the G-d of love and leave all loving to Him, retaining vengeance for yourselves."

◆§ Was It Really an Exaggeration?

R' Menachem Mendel of Lubavitch was once summoned by one of the ministers of the Czarist government. The minister, who obviously had "studied" Judaism, heaped scorn on the *Gemara* in general. "How can you Jews accept a book filled with such items?" he asked. "Take, for example, the story of a bird's egg which exploded, releasing a flood which destroyed sixty towns and uprooted three hundred cedar trees (*Bechoros* 57). How can you treat such a book as holy?"

"Your excellency," replied R' Menachem Mendel, explaining it on a level the minister could comprehend, "as you know, your government issued a law recently which forced all the Jews in Russia to live in the Pale of Settlement — one small section of the country. Those Jews living outside it are now being forced to pack up whatever they have and to move. This affects Jews in no fewer than six hundred towns and villages. Now, let us say I'm a historian writing an account of this. I am extremely upset by the action and wish to express my own view in this account, but I know that if I do, the authorities will not permit my book to be published. I can therefore write about this magnificent Czar, who, with but a drop of ink, caused six hundred towns and villages to be flooded. In future years, those who have forgotten the cause of this account will read it and declare it to be absurd.

"Your excellency," he concluded,"we are distanced from these events by hundreds of years, and are totally unaware of the background leading up to this account. Though it appears to make no sense whatsoever, those who lived through the events depicted here knew precisely to what these stories referred."

⋑ What Excuse Can I Have?

R' Meir of Kobrin had a very sweet disposition. He could be hurt by others, but never responded in kind. Once, his chassidim asked him: "Rebbe, *Chazal* tell us that every *talmid chacham* who does not exact retribution is not truly a *talmid chacham*, so why do you act the way you do?"

"The reason is simple," said R' Meir. "When I come to the next world, if I take revenge and exact retribution in this world, they may criticize me for having done so. Now what can I tell them in my defense — that I'm a *talmid chacham*? And what happens if they disagree? What can I possibly say to justify my actions? If, on the other hand, I do not take revenge in this world and am criticized in the next world for not having done so, I have a simple defense: I can always claim I didn't know I was a *talmid chacham*."

⋑ Who Is Whose Slave?

R' Zvi Hirsh of Safrin was a disciple of the *Chozeh* of Lublin, but he also went to other rebbes to learn from them the different qualities in which they excelled. Once, when R' Zvi Hirsh was about to leave the *Chozeh*, he realized that he had no money, so he asked the *Chozeh* for a loan. The *Chozeh* lent him the money, but added joyfully, "Now you are completely mine, because the *Gemara* says that a borrower is the slave of the lender."

"On the contrary," said R' Zvi Hirsh, "now you're mine, because the *Gemara* also says that a person who acquires a slave for himself thereby acquires a master for himself."

⋑ You Cannot Expect More

Once, a garrison of Austrian troops came to the town of Rimanov. The soldiers looked for a place large enough to store all their weapons and provisions, and after surveying all the buildings in town decided that the only suitable building was the town *shul*. They quickly issued orders to have the *shul* expropriated for their entire stay.

When the Jews found out about the edict, they convened an emergency meeting with their *rav*, R' Mendele, to try to find some way to annul the order. As they were discussing the issue, one of the leaders of the community offered some possible ray of comfort. "When they examine the building carefully," he said, "they will realize that the walls are so dilapidated that they're in danger of collapsing at any minute. Add to that the fact that the roof leaks like a sieve, they may even decide that the building is totally unsuitable for their needs."

When R' Mendele heard this comment, he exclaimed: "Up to this moment, I was puzzled as to why we should have to suffer this terrible decree. What had we done that made us worthy of such punishment by Hashem? Now I've finally realized the cause of it all. If we ourselves don't care about the state of our *shul*, why should Hashem care about it?

"The way to avert the decree," he went on, "is for us to start working this very day on repairing whatever has to be fixed in the *shul*. We have to engage the workers needed to take care of everything in need of repair. And as soon as the repairs have been completed, we have to repaint the *shul*, so that it is a place which offers glory to Hashem."

The townsfolk accepted R' Mendele's rebuke, and immediately began to work on fixing up the *shul*. In a short time, they had restored it to its original beauty.

Not long after, the military officers came back to the town, examined the *shul* again, and decided that it was too small for their needs. Instead, they decided to move their troops to a neighboring town, where they could find a larger building for their purposes.

ৎৡ You Have Accomplished Your Purpose

The *Chafetz Chaim* once asked a certain *maggid* to speak to a group about the prohibition against *lashon hara*. When the *maggid* returned, he told the *Chafetz Chaim*, "I spoke to them for two hours on the topic, but I doubt if I accomplished anything."

"That's not true," said the *Chafetz Chaim*. "At the very least, during the two hours they listened to you, no one spoke *lashon hara*."

ৎৡ You're the Master of the House

R' Yehoshua Zeitlin, in addition to being a very great Torah scholar, was known for his brilliant thinking in worldly affairs. It is said that the Russian minister Potemkin would come to him to seek his advice on various matters of state.

Once Potemkin came to R' Yehoshua to discuss an important matter. As soon as he entered R' Yehoshua's home, R' Yehoshua stood up to greet him and remained standing. He did not offer the minister a chair. After they had been standing and talking for half an hour, the minister, who was already tired, asked him: "Rabbi, how is it that I have been here for half an hour and that you, as the master of the house, didn't offer me a seat?"

"Your excellency," replied R' Yehoshua, "as a minister of the Russian court, wherever you are you're the master of the house."

ৎৡ Only Pebbles

In a battle between various factions of Jews, a rock was thrown at the window of R' Yom Tov Lipa Teitelbaum and barely missed the rebbe. When his chassidim saw this, they exclaimed: "See how evil some people are. That stone could have caused serious injury!"

R' Yom Tov Lipa, however, had a different explanation: "No Jew could possibly have thrown such a large rock that would endanger other Jews. What happened is that a number of Jews threw small little pebbles, but in flight the pebbles all stated, 'Let me rest on the righteous one's head' (see *Rashi* to *Bereishis* 28:11). As a result, all the little pebbles coalesced into a single large rock, and that was what came smashing through the window."

A Matter of Perspective

◄§ *A Topsy-Turvy World*

R' Moshe of Kuznitz said, "I really don't understand the way people think. When a person is poor or sick or in some other distress, he invariably blames Hashem and not himself for his condition. On the other hand, when he becomes rich or succeeds in some other way, he never attributes his success to Hashem's help, but rather takes full credit."

◄§ *How To Read It Correctly*

A man came to the *Chazon Ish* and complained that he had no source of income to support his family. Furthermore, he pointed out, the *Gemara* states clearly, "Not (לא in Hebrew) every day does a miracle occur."

"The problem," said the *Chazon Ish*, "is that you're reading the *Gemara* incorrectly. You should read it: 'No (לא) — every day a miracle occurs.'"

❧ Smaller Than a Word

R' Moshe of Kobrin was once addressing his disciples and told them that when one prays his entire body must enter into each word.

"But Rebbe," argued one of his listeners, "how can one fit the entire human body into a single small word?"

"I'm only referring to a person who feels himself smaller than even the smallest word," repled R' Moshe. "This doesn't apply to anyone who thinks himself bigger than a word."

❧ Looking at the Proper Place

When R' Eizel Charif became the *rav* of Kutno he was very young and many opposed his appointment on the grounds of his youth. A congregant once criticised him by noting that his *Shemoneh Esrei* was much shorter than that of the town's previous *rav*. "I, am used to the members of my community looking toward heaven when they pray, rather than to the feet of the *rav*," R' Eizel replied.

❧ Opening the Hearts

R' Aharon of Karlin once broke into tears and cried out, "How I wish I had a key which would open up all the hearts that are stopped up!"

A chassid who was there said to him, "Rebbe, when one doesn't have a key, one breaks in by using a sharp point." R' Aharon praised the man highly for his comment.

❧ Even a Key May Not Be Enough

R' Yaakov David of Slutzk was known throughout Europe as a *darshan*, who frequently brought his audience to tears with his words.

He was once invited to speak before the community in Kurland on *Shabbos Shuvah* — the Shabbos before Yom Kippur. The people of Kurland included many who were far from God-fearing, and R' Yaakov David's impassioned speech rolled off the backs of the congregants.

Later, when R' Yaakov David was asked why this brilliant speech had made so little impact, he replied, "It is my task to use the right key to open the faucet. If, however, the barrel that we are trying to fill is empty, it doesn't make a difference how much the faucet has been opened."

❧ Owned by a Thief

One of the duties of R' Eizel Charif was to check the weights used by the local merchants to ensure that people received their full measure when they bought anything. This inspection took place each Monday and Thursday. A local merchant once told him, "Rebbe, I simply don't have time to check my weights twice a week. I'm a very busy man."

"That's fine," said R' Eizel. "I am quite willing to dispense with checking your weights on one condition — that in the front of your store you hang a sign proclaiming: 'This store is owned by a thief.' "

❧ Priorities

R' Nosson of Makova was once approached by the residents of a certain town, who were in the process of selecting a *rav.* There were two candidates. One was very learned in both Torah and secular studies. The other was not as learned in Torah and knew nothing of secular studies, but was much more pious. Whom should they choose?

R' Nosson decided immediately in favor of the second. "The Torah," he said, "states that when we choose judges for ourselves, they are to be as 'Hashem your God gives you,' namely men who will instill reverence for Hashem, for only they offer 'true justice.'

"Furthermore," Reb Nosson added, "if you have any hesitation about appointing such a man because you are afraid that people will not respect him for his lack of a secular education, *Chazal* assure us that 'Every person who has true fear of Heaven is obeyed.'"

◆§ Step by Step

R' Rafael of Barshad once warned his chassidim against the evils of theft and deception. One of the chassidim seemed very distraught, and R' Rafael later called him aside and asked him, "Did I say anything to offend you?"

"My job is selling fish," the man replied. "If I didn't tell lies here and there, I would never be able to make a living."

"If that is the case," said R' Rafael, "I want you to promise me that you will never deceive anyone if all you stand to gain is a kopek or less." "That I promise," said the man. "From now on, I will never lie for the gain of a kopek." Some time later, after the man had become used to not lying over a kopek, R' Rafael extended the ban to two kopeks, and so on, until the man stopped lying altogether.

◆§ The Exact Opposite

R' Menachem Mendel of Kotzk once remarked, "It is strange how, when people disagree with a great individual, they accuse him of things which are the exact opposite of the truth. So it was even with Moshe Rabbeinu. Though he was 'the most humble of men,' Korach accused him of 'seeking to rule over the congregation of Hashem.'"

ᴥ§ *True Justice*

A non-Jew once discussed with R' Avraham Yehoshua of Apta the different rules governing legal procedures. "With us," he said, "when there is a case involving two litigants, the trial date is set far in advance. That way, the people have time to prepare their cases. Then, when the case comes up for trial before a judge, each litigant is represented by a lawyer. Even if a person loses his case, he can still appeal it to a higher court. With you, on the other hand, in every small village, as soon as two people quarrel, they immediately go to the rabbi. The rabbi hears both sides, and in most cases renders the verdict on the spot. Where's the justice? Isn't our way far superior?"

"Let me tell you a story," said R' Avraham Yehoshua. "A wolf once managed to kill a deer. As it started to eat the deer, along came a lion and snatched the deer away. The wolf ran to the fox, asking him to judge the case. The wolf, of course, had a simple claim: he had been the one to kill the deer. The lion, as opposed to this, claimed that as king of the beasts he was entitled to have the deer. The fox listened to both sides, and then ruled: "You both have a good point. I will divide the carcass, and each of you will receive a half.'

"No sooner said than done. The fox took the carcass and divided in half — but not quite in half. One side was bigger than the other. 'We'll soon settle that,' said the fox, biting a hunk off the larger side and eating it. But he had bitten off too much, and now the other side was larger. Again he had to chew off a chunk. Finally, by the time the two sides were equal, there was nothing but bones left for the lion and the wolf.

"And the same is true with your court cases," concluded R' Avraham Yehoshua. "By the time the case is finally settled and all the lawyers paid off, there's nothing left for either litigant."

✑ Two Ways of Looking at Thinking

R' Avraham of Bobroisk, a Lubavitch chassid, was asked to explain how it is that some people who serve Hashem in every way are depressed their entire lives, while others, who serve Hashem just as well, are always joyful. He explained as follows: "The former looks at where the soul was before it came down to the earth, and how low it has sunk since then. As a result he is despondent. The joyful person on the other hand, looks at where the soul is now and where it will ultimately go, and that is why he is always happy.

"Despondency," he added, "has a role to play in causing a person who has sinned to repent his ways. But it is a very strong medicine, and a person who takes this medicine all the time, even when it is not necessary, will find that it doesn't help him. Joy, on the other hand, is a medicine which a person can take his entire life, especially if the joy is based on one's delight in serving Hashem."

✑ What Do We Do With Our Mitzvos?

Two followers of the Dubno *Maggid* were talking. One remarked, "I don't know what will become of us with all the sins we've committed."

"My sins don't concern me," replied the other, "because it is always possible to do *teshuvah* and repent one's sins. What bothers me is the *mitzvos* I have performed. How can I come before Hashem with *mitzvos* such as these?"

✑ What Will I Say?

When R' Menachem Mendel of Vitebsk was appointed to head the community of Minsk, a large reception was held in his honor and his contract as *rav* read aloud. When R' Menachem Mendel got up to speak, he told the members of the community, "How fortunate I will be, after 120 years, when I come to the World-to-Come. I will be able to produce the invitation you sent me, which is full of praise and all types of fancy titles. I will thus be able to bring evidence that the people of Minsk think I am a *gaon* and a *tzaddik* and so on. However, they will then ask me, 'Mendel, do you agree with what is written here?' Then I won't be able to say anything in my defense."

ക You're Absolutely Right

A *chazan* once boasted to R' Abush of Frankfurt that his prayers were so powerful that immediately after the *Geshem* ("Rain") prayer on *Shemini Atzeres,* the skies had become overcast and it had rained.

R' Abush, who knew the *chazan* to be far from virtuous in his religious observance, said, "You're absolutely right. People like you indeed bring rain to the world. In fact they can even bring about a flood."

ക You're Undoing My Life's Work

When R' Benzion of Bobov came to Cracow, his enthusiastic chassidim wanted to unharness the horses pulling his carriage and pull the carriage themselves.

R' Benzion said to them, "My entire life I have spent trying to convert horses into human beings, and now you are trying to convert human beings into horses."

ക It's My Fault

R' Elimelech of Lizhensk once asked his son, "Do you know why so many people come to me and demand that I bless them with good health and sustenance? I assume it is because they know that I am responsible for their troubles for it is my sins that have tipped the balance of the world to the negative side."

❧ Is There Any Bad?

A chassid asked the *Chozeh* of Lublin, "Rebbe, the *Mishnah* states that a person has to recite a blessing even when something bad occurs to him. And the *Gemara* adds that not only must he recite a blessing, he must rejoice and accept with joy whatever happens to him. I don't understand the *Gemara*. How is it possible to rejoice over something bad?"

The *Chozeh* answered him, "You don't understand the *Gemara*, but I don't understand the *Mishnah*. How can the *Mishnah* say that one must rejoice over the bad? Is there any bad in the world?"

❧ It Depends on How You Look at It

R' Yosef Yozl Horowitz of Novardhok used to say: "If you come to the train station and find that the train has left, don't say that you were late for the previous train, but that you're early for the next one. Everything is in Hashem's hands."

❧ A Rich Man Among Rich Men

R' Shimon the *Maggid* was once invited to address a certain community and offer guidance in what the townspeople could do to improve themselves. "I'm willing to do so," said R' Shimon, "provided the community arranges a loan of fifty thousand rubles for three days, to be repaid the day after my address." As R' Shimon was known everywhere as a scrupulously honest man, the community elders had no problem raising the required amount.

R' Shimon delivered a discourse the likes of which had never been heard before. Everyone was moved to tears, and all pledged themselves to improve in their ways, both between man and man and between man and Hashem.

The next day, R' Shimon returned fifty thousand rubles. The elders of the community were surprised to see that he gave back the same exact notes and coins he had borrowed three days earlier, and asked R' Shimon for an explanation.

"You see," said R' Shimon, "a poor man is naturally intimidated by the wealthy, and I was afraid that in my speech I might not have the courage to castigate the rich for their wrongs. With fifty thousand rubles in my possession, I felt absolutely no compunctions about castigating anyone."

⋅᠍§ *Too High*

A visitor once attended a Torah discourse given by the *Maggid* of Mezritch. At the conclusion of the discourse, R' Shneur Zalman, the *Maggid's* disciple, turned to the visitor and asked him what he thought of what he had heard. "To tell you the truth, Rebbe," replied the man, "I found it difficult to follow the discourse, because the *Maggid's* voice was so low."

"I, too, found it difficult to follow the discourse," said R' Shneur Zalman, "but to me the problem was that what the *Maggid* says is so high."

This volume is part of
THE ARTSCROLL SERIES®
an ongoing project of
translations, commentaries and expositions
on Scripture, Mishnah, Talmud, Halachah,
liturgy, history and the classic Rabbinic writings;
and biographies, and thought.

For a brochure of current publications
visit your local Hebrew bookseller
or contact the publisher:

Mesorah Publications, ltd

4401 Second Avenue
Brooklyn, New York 11232
(718) 921-9000